AF470387

NORFOLK
A GHOSTHUNTER'S GUIDE

Norfolk

A Ghosthunter's Guide

Neil R. Storey

COUNTRYSIDE BOOKS
NEWBURY, BERKSHIRE

For Molly

Designed by Peter Davies, Nautilus Design
Produced through MRM Associates Ltd., Reading
Typeset by Jean Cussons Typesetting, Diss, Norfolk
Printed by Cambridge University Press

•Contents•

CONTENTS

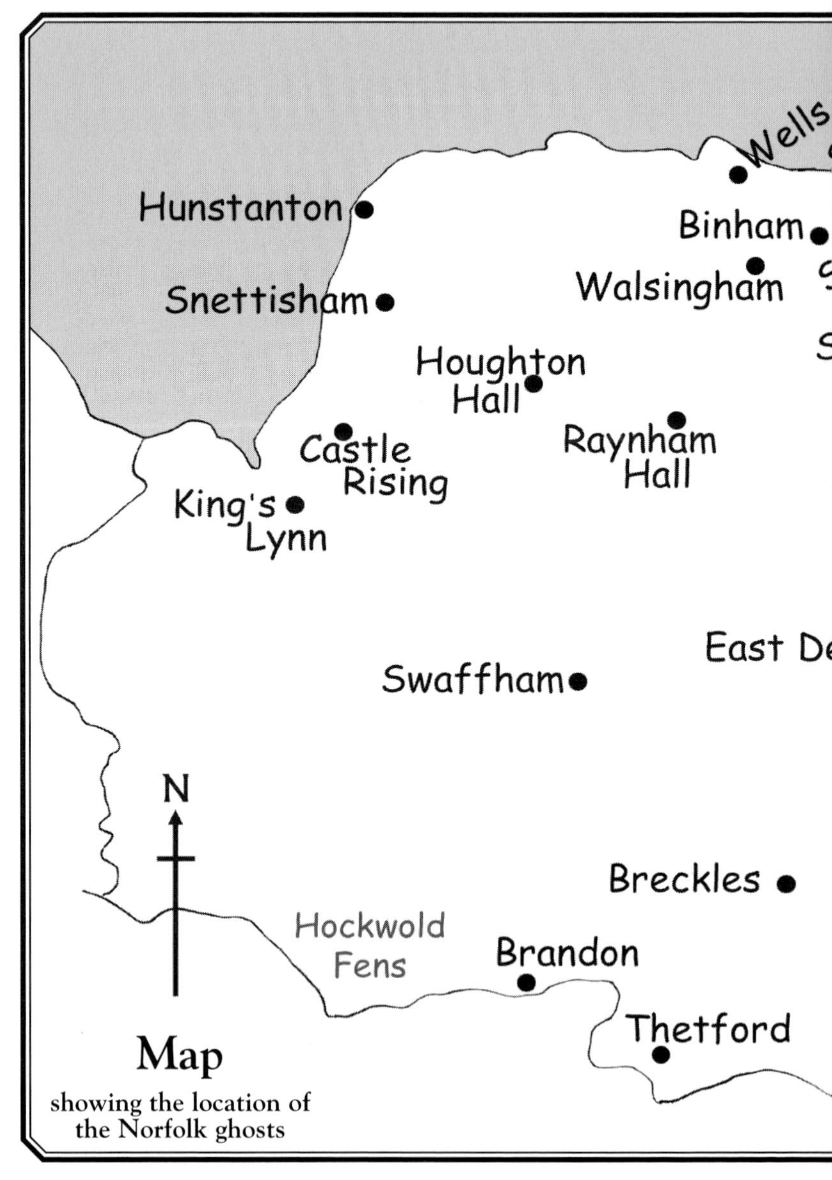

Map

showing the location of the Norfolk ghosts

Cley
Weybourne
Sheringham
Cromer
Overstrand
Mundesley
Aylmerton
Felbrigg Hall
Bacton
Happisburgh
Swafield
rpe
NorthWalsham
Ingham
Aylsham
Waxham
ston
Worstead
Hickling
Irstead
Coltishall
Potter Heigham
Ludham
Hemsby
Salhouse
Acle
Gt Yarmouth
Melton
Norwich
Burgh Castle
Loddon
Shotesham
Thurlton
Burgh St Peter

• Introduction •

I f you believe the old English tradition that says the spirit of the
first person buried in any graveyard becomes its sentinel and
guards it against the darker forces of the night then, because
Norfolk has the greatest concentration of medieval churches (and
thus graveyards) in Europe, we must have the greatest number of
ghosts right here in this great county.

Add in the number of white ladies, lantern men, ghosts, shades
and poltergeists reported from Norfolk over the years and nowhere
else comes close. The trouble is that in many cases these spirits
have no clear history beyond a brief mention in the folklore of the
district. This could be attributed to the reaction of most true sons
of Norfolk who, typically, have no truck with ghosts, or at least
that might be the first impression a stranger to the county gets;
hence in many ghost books other counties seem to have a
preponderance of paranormal activity.

But, as we say in these parts, 'Hold yew hard, bor.' I have often
found when researching some of the darker aspects of the county's
history that just below the surface, in the more dusty boxes or
volumes, there is plenty of material for the paranormal
investigator. Armed with careful research, and taking the time to
visit the sites and to have a mardle with a few of the locals, it is
soon apparent that belief in and witnesses to the paranormal in
this county are still widespread. I have also been fortunate to
gain many useful stories and leads from the readers of my column
in the *Norfolk Journal*, and also as I go around the county lecturing,
especially after my appearance on a number of TV programmes
and documentaries about the paranormal, including *Most
Haunted*.

I hope that all you ghosthunters out there will find this volume helpful. Over the years, and most particularly during the research for this book, my family and I have had great fun ghosthunting and have visited some fascinating places. I have tried to guide you to the more difficult locations with OS map references but please be aware some of the houses mentioned are not just 'private property' but people's homes, so I ask you to please respect their privacy.

While compiling this volume, I have been faced with far too many tales, indeed enough to fill another book, so on this occasion I have chosen my personal favourites from across Norfolk. Some will probably be known to you, but I hope I will bring a few lesser known facts or more modern twists and postscripts to the stories. As many Norfolk tales are a heady mix of legend and ghosts, I have tried to base these on the earliest or, what seems to me, the most reliable account. But, dear reader, it is still up to your judgement and discretion to decide what is long-embroidered legend or real evidence of the paranormal.

Happy ghosthunting and good luck!

Neil R. Storey

AYLMERTON
The Shrieking Pits

In the woods near Roman Camp (OS Explorer 252: GR 1840) there is a series of shallow depressions believed to be ironworking pits dating from about AD 1000. Possibly because of an unusual combination of these landscape features and gradients with strong winds from off the sea, this area became known as the shrieking pits. According to local legend, though, there may be another cause of the eerie wails heard in this area.

The story tells of how a wicked man killed both his wife and babe in a fit of anger and buried them in separate pits. The ghost of the mother, still in the ankle-length white nightdress she was wearing when she was killed, moves from pit to pit on stormy nights, clearly distressed, wringing her hands, wailing and calling for her lost child.

Similar ancient pits can be found over much of the West Runton Heath and Aylmerton area. Down past Aylmerton church, on the meadows to the west before the iron railings, there are water-filled depressions (GR 180399) and the spectre of the woman in white has also been reported here (see *Norfolk Ghosts & Legends* by Polly Howat). When researching this book I took three photographs with my digital camera across these peaceful green meadows. The weather was fine, clear and dry but when I checked the pictures on the preview screen one of them showed a strange orb clearly hovering over above one of these pools. My partner Molly was with me and neither of us had seen anything that might

The eerie woods and pits of Aylmerton.

have caused the strange image to appear in the shot. There was no evidence of dust on the lens and there was no indication of a similar orb or mark on the previous or subsequent pictures. Perhaps the White Lady is still making her presence known.

Aylsham District and Blickling Hall
Anne Boleyn and the Headless Horseman

As a lad growing up in North Norfolk, one of the first ghost stories I ever heard was that concerning Anne Boleyn. Married in secret to King Henry VIII in January 1533, Anne Boleyn, daughter of Sir Thomas Boleyn of Norfolk's Blicking Hall, was Henry's second wife. To marry her Henry had to divorce Catherine of Aragon, thus causing the schism with the Roman Catholic Church that provided the occasion for the official Reformation in England. Anne fell pregnant and presented King Henry with a fine daughter who grew up to become Elizabeth I, but this was not the son and heir the King so desired and she fell out of favour when she miscarried a son. On trumped-up charges of adultery, with allegations of witchcraft in reserve, Anne was sentenced to be beheaded and this was carried out on 19th May 1536. She was granted the favour of having the headsman of her choice and an expert with the sword was sent for from Calais. He executed her as she knelt upright; his assistant made a noise to cause her to turn her head and, with the neck so exposed, the executioner completed his bloody duty with one sweep of his sword. Tragic Anne was buried upright in an arrow chest in St Peter ad Vincula Chapel within the walls of the Tower of London. Her spirit could not sleep soundly, though, and upon every anniversary of her execution, her ghost, bathed in an eerie

The pits in the fields opposite Aylmerton church. Is the strange 'orb' above the pond a trick of the light or a manifestation of the tragic wailing woman in white?

blue light, her neck a raw stump oozing blood and her head on her lap, was reported to have struck terror into locals around the Aylsham and Blicking area. It travelled at breakneck speed in a spectral carriage, drawn by headless horses and driven by a headless horseman, and made its way to its final destination at Blickling Hall. Here the carriage would clatter up the drive and disappear just before it reached the hall.

In a variation of the tale, Sir Thomas Boleyn, the unfortunate father of Anne, was said to have been condemned to drive the spectral coach containing his headless daughter for 1,000 years. With the reins for the headless horses in one hand, his own decapitated head belching fire tucked under the other arm, he whips the coach up over twelve bridges in the vicinity, including Aylsham, Burgh, Oxnead, Buxton, Coltishall (being careful to avoid Black Shuck as he crosses this bridge at midnight) as well as 'the two Meyton bridges, Wroxham and two others' – and all this before cock-crow! But then, in particularly fanciful accounts, he is also chased by a pack of the Devil's own hounds, whipped on by demons. This tale was accompanied by a warning that Sir Thomas's disembodied head may cry out for you to open a gate for the coach. Anyone fool enough to do as requested, make a reply or give any indication that they heard the request would risk being carried off with the coach and down to hell itself.

Perhaps this particularly horrible version of the tale was a convenient cover for smugglers running their contraband inland. On moonlit nights they would remove their driver's hat, blacken his face and turn up his collar – thus creating a headless coachman. They would then take a white horse and paint its head black, so it, too, became headless. With this vision clattering along the road, would superstitious locals hang around to see if it was the real thing and risk being dragged off to hell?

The magnificent Blickling Hall is, in fact, Jacobean and was not the one that would have been known to Anne Boleyn. The old

The magnificent Blickling Hall.

---

hall was built nearer the lake and it is there that a curious postscript may be found to this story. Before the house was put in the hands of the National Trust, it was the home of Lord Lothian. Shortly before the Second World War his lordship's butler, Sidney Hancock, a very down-to-earth man, was one of a few staff in the house late one night when he looked out of a window and noticed the figure of a woman walking along the edge of the lake. Sidney wondered what she was doing there and left the house to investigate. As he approached her, Sidney observed her curiously old-fashioned white collar and cap. He enquired, 'Excuse me, are you looking for somebody?' to which she replied, 'That for which I seek has long since gone.' Somewhat bemused by the reply and rather than stare at the woman Sidney dropped his head for a moment. He was about to speak to her again but when he looked up – she had vanished.

Perhaps this sad and lonely figure was Anne, or maybe she is another spirit altogether, the hall's resident spook known to staff as the 'Grey Lady'. Denis Mead, who retired as house manager, having been associated with Blickling Hall for over 40 years, describes her as 'accepted by those of us who work here as being one of the family'. This spectre wears a long grey dress with a white lace collar and a white cap, and has been spotted in the long gallery library, apparently looking at books, as well as in the dining room and on the stairs. Inexperienced members of staff that have approached her, ready to respectfully ask her to return to the public side of the guide ropes, find, as they move to approach her, that she just fades away.

But what of the phantom carriage? Was it just a ruse or is there more to it? Well, it is recorded that Constance, Marchioness of Lothian (1836–1901) when resident at Blickling would never look out of her window on the night of 19th May for fear of what she might see. However, 'she would never be able to sleep until she heard the carriage wheels on the gravel of the driveway'.

A final twist to this tale comes from a gentleman who introduced himself to me after one of my talks. His experience goes back to the mid 1960s when the man, whom I shall call Ken, was a young and inexperienced driver travelling late at night on the road from Aylsham past Blickling Hall. It was raining and fairly blustery; admittedly his senses were heightened on this winding route where the old trees creaked and groaned as their arm-like branches lunged and dipped overhead in the wind. Quite suddenly, only a short distance past the entrance to the main drive

Queen Anne Boleyn.

up to the hall and without any visual or aural warning, Ken was overcome by an irresistible urge to pull off the road in an emergency manoeuvre, which caused his car to hit the embankment with such force it almost turned over. As he wrenched the wheel Ken saw what he could only describe as a 'large black mass' on the road, speeding past his car. One question lingers on in Ken's mind about that accident; was it just the sound of the car juddering to an abrupt halt or was it really hooves he heard as the manifestation passed into the distance? I shall leave you to decide, but I will add that the date on the old insurance claim form he showed me was 19th May 1966 – the 430th anniversary of the execution of Queen Anne Boleyn.

BACTON TO MUNDESLEY COASTAL PATH
The Lone Coastguardsman

In the early 19th century the Norfolk coast was rife with smuggling operations, which brought in all manner of exotic goods from tea and tobacco to lace and Genever. The Revenue cutter *Ranger* sailed out from Yarmouth on regular night-time patrols at sea while customs officers had bases and patrol areas along the entire coast. Many people disliked and did not trust the Customs officers and gladly worked against them. Millers across the marshes and all along the coast would drop their sails to an agreed position when the Revenue boat sailed out and by this windmill-sail semaphore the warning message normally reached the smugglers in just enough time for them to make their escape. If the Revenue men did make a seizure it could cost the smugglers dearly; for example, in 1817 *Ranger* under the command of Captain Sayers captured a large lugger with an armed crew of 36

The cliff line between Mundesley and Bacton. Does the lone coastguardsman still walk this lonely path after dark?

men. The cargo consisted of 507 ankers and 945 halves of spirits, 27 bales of tobacco and 47 bales of Bandannnas (sic), the whole worth £8,000.

If smugglers were caught, it was more often due to then ill-luck or from the word of one who had turned informer. This latter path was incredibly dangerous. If you were discovered as the one who had betrayed the smugglers, you could well be dragged from your bed in the middle of the night, whipped in the street and bundled onto the back of a horse, or dragged behind it, and your body never seen again. One coastguardsman thought he had tamed an informer and strode out along the cliff path between Bacton and Mundesley to intercept a smuggling band. Having sent a boy to summon the local troop of yeomanry for back-up, he went to the agreed place and shone his lamp to lead the smugglers into the trap. What he did not realise was that the boy was in the pay of the smugglers, no troops would be coming and the lamp he was carrying would simply lead the smugglers to him.

When the shadowy shapes of the smugglers started to bob along the moonlit beach, the coastguardsman, being a tall and well-built man and thinking that the troopers would be in position, shouted as he ran forward to lead the attack. He was alone, the smugglers were many; the coastguardsman was mercilessly cut to pieces and his body parts flung over the cliff edge and washed out to sea. Ending his days in such a horrific way and having no grave, and with all his body parts not even being in the same place, the lone coastguardsman was doomed to walk the coastal path between Bacton and Mundesley for ever more. He manifests on moonless and stormy nights when he sings and shouts at the top of his voice above the howl of the wind and the crash of the waves. During lulls you may hear him laugh loudly. On quieter nights his calls and screams for help have been heard, but they always sound a long way off. Much of the coastguardsman's old coastal path 'walk' has been eroded over time but in recent years people in neighbouring caravan parks have occasionally spoken of mysterious lights floating by, perhaps the lantern of the coastguardsman as he passes on his lonely walk.

BINHAM
The Fiddler and His Dog

One tale that has been recorded at Binham for a good few generations begins with the legend that a tunnel used to run all the way from the Benedictine priory there to

Walsingham, and, what was more, the tunnel was haunted by a tall 'Black Monk' who also walked along the length of the tunnel above ground on moonless nights. As the figure moved he appeared to be shaking his hooded head and peering around as if he had mislaid something. Over the years there were cave-ins, also cuts made into the tunnel at various points with the intention of searching it for hidden treasure or just to find out if it really did go all the way to Walsingham, but each time local folks were deterred from exploring too far by a 'menacing presence' and a fear that 'the Black Monk would get them'.

One day, about 300 years ago, part of the old tunnel collapsed and an opening was revealed near the priory. Many of the locals came to peer in and have a poke around in the areas lit by daylight – but no further. Finally, one Jimmy Griggs came over and said that he would investigate the tunnel with his dog, Trap, for company and the rest of the locals could follow his progress above ground. Jimmy suggested that he should play his fiddle as he went along so they could keep track of him. He seemed to be going along well enough and the locals were beginning to enjoy the excitement until, judging by the sound of the violin, he had reached the barrow now known as Fiddler's Hill (OS Explorer 251: GR 961410). Abruptly the music ended. Some put their ears to the ground, while others got back to the entrance hole as fast as they could and shouted to Jimmy, but all was silent and neither Jimmy nor his dog were ever seen alive again. J. Wentworth Day in his book *Ghosts and Witches* points out: 'Oddly enough, when the county council workmen were excavating at a place called Fiddler's Hill in April 1935, they discovered the skeletons of a man and a dog, which I understand, were verified by Dr Hicks of Wells-next-the-Sea.'

It seems the Black Monk has not put an appearance along the tunnel for some years but Binham Priory remains a place of unexplained presences and emotions. Numerous people have told

The ruins of Binham Priory. Perhaps the lost spirit of the Black Monk still lingers here.

me of an uncomfortable sensation of 'something' or a 'presence' near them or a feeling that they were 'being watched' while visiting the ruins. I was once told, quite insistently, by an old native of the area as he looked me in the eye that 'suffun wunt right up that priory – there's suffun what need to be laid to rest good'n proper there by a minister or someone who really know what they're doin'. Sadly he would not elaborate any further but I was left in no doubt that he had seen or experienced something there and was being deadly serious.

One family was visiting the priory in the early 1980s and although the day was overcast there was nothing obviously untoward, but one by one they all confided that they didn't like the feeling that pervaded the place. One of the group, a plain-thinking and normally easy-going Norfolk man in his 70s who had served in the Far East and had experienced the horror of jungle warfare first hand, said he had 'never felt an atmosphere anything like it'. He was adamant that they should leave, and the rest of the family did not need any persuasion to go. Could it be that the Black Monk is still making his malevolent presence known at Binham Priory?

CAWSTON
Duel to the Death

A duel was fought on Cawston Heath on 20th August 1698 between Sir Henry Hobart, the 4th Baronet of Blickling Hall, and Oliver Le Neve of Great Witchingham Hall, as the result of quarrel following the election of Hobart's rival, Le Neve, to be Member of Parliament for Norwich in his place. After the opening formalities swords were drawn and the duel commenced. Sir Henry had the best of the fight until a carefully delivered thrust saw Le Neve run him through his belly, and he retired from the field, mortally wounded. Support for Hobart was so strong that Le Neve fled to Holland but subsequently returned, stood trial and was acquitted.

A stone pillar and urn, carved with the initials 'H H', still stands on the site about a mile from Cawston on the old heath where the duel took place (OS Explorer 238: GR 153240). Over the years the sound of the fatal clash of swords has been heard from the tiny green that is preserved around the site of the monument. A hedge and a few oak trees surround this area. In the spring it is carpeted by an impressive display of white crocus. I have visited this site on

The duel stone at Cawston.

a number of occasions, both alone and with my groups of students, at a variety of times of year. A busy road passes nearby but, whether you know the details of this place or not, when you pass though the entrance gate many feel there is a palpable change of atmosphere – not evil, not a presence but a sense that people simply describe as 'odd', 'cold' and 'not quite of our time'. Go with an open mind, perhaps take someone who does not know the story, and see what you both make of it.

To conclude the account, Sir Henry was removed from the scene of the duel to his family home at Blicking Hall where he died of his wound the following day in the west turret bedchamber. His groans are said to still haunt the room on the anniversary of his death. Even when no sounds are heard the room has been said to have an 'odd' atmosphere. One member of staff had a dog that simply would not enter the room and would stand at the door baring its teeth, growling, with its hackles raised. During the Second World War Blickling Hall was commandeered by the RAF and the commanding officer occupied this particular room. Although he was a man who would not countenance the existence of the spirit world, neither he nor anyone else could explain why it was nigh on impossible to keep all three doors of the room shut at the same time.

CROMER AND SHERINGHAM
Shipden Bells and the Cries
of Drowned Sailors

Shipden, the lost town that once stood on the seaward side of Cromer, is recorded in the Domesday Book. As with many places swept away by time and tide, its prominence has become exaggerated by folk tales and mythology. This is evinced by S. J. Pratt in his book, *To the Sea*, where he writes of Shipden's 'flocks, herds, spires, turrets and battlements'.

Shipden was a typical North Norfolk trading port and by the 14th century it was a well-populated town, with a harbour and a number of manors, but it suffered a constant fight with encroachments by the sea. By 1337, great chunks had been bitten out of it, and the church, which was dedicated to St Peter, was abandoned to decay by the 1340s. Shipden's trade moved to its landward satellite of Cromer and eventually the town was eaten away by the indefatigable lap and crash of the waves – but that was not going to be the last we heard of it.

*Cromer Pier. Cup your hand to your ear and you may hear
the Shipden bells booming below the waves.*

All the fishermen of this area are aware of the lost village of Shipden, especially the ruinous 'church rock' just beyond the pier, which is a notorious sea hazard. On 9th August 1888 the pleasure steamer *Victoria* had set out on an unwise course from the pier and scraped over 'church rock', holing her port side. Fortunately she did not sink and all passengers were ferried off and sent home by train. Surely this is the only instance of a ship being stranded on the top of a church tower! Many is the time the hardiest of fishermen have cupped their hands to their ears to check that the fabled bells of Shipden church were not booming from its submerged belfry – for if they were, only a fool would go to sea that day because a storm would be brewing. Perhaps they would also listen for the 'Yow-Yows', thought to be the ghostly calls of drowned fishermen and sailors warning their mortal compatriots at Cromer and Sheringham of danger at sea. In the waters off Sheringham it was said that the disembodied shouts of a phantom ship's captain who drowned there could occasionally be heard. On numerous occasions fishermen would hear the sounds coming up off the water and rowed to the calls to bring help to what sounded like the desperate cries of a drowning man. When they got near, the shouts would suddenly seem to come from the opposite direction and if the fishermen did not take the warning the sounds would emanate from directly below the boat – and if you heard that you knew you would have to row to the shore for all your life was worth to avoid the imminent squall that would surely follow.

The most effective places to hear the calls or 'Yow-Yows' on land are on the higher ground away from the modern attractions of the holidaymaker's seaside resorts. Be careful, however, if you are near the parish boundary of Sheringham, close to one of the old fisherman's gaps, for you may hear the sound of stones slowly falling one by one on a big rock. This sound is said to be the ghostly reminder of where the bodies of twelve drowned sailors, who had been washed up on the beach, were buried without Christian rites and simply covered with a pile of pebbles. Another good place to catch the call of the 'Yow-Yows' is directly above the sea waters on Cromer pier.

It is also on the pier that the shady figures of long gone fishermen, who were quite probably also lifeboatmen, linger near the No 1 lifeboat house at the pier head. Sometimes their spirits are also known to wander around the theatre. Perhaps these old salts were shanty men as there are regular accounts of male voices who join in or take the male lines in songs being rehearsed and performed in the theatre. It is also suggested that the spirit of the affectionately remembered impresario and manager of the Norwich Theatre Royal, Dick Condon, who loved the Cromer

Felbrigg Hall, once home to generations of the Windham family,
now a National Trust property open to the public.

Pavilion so, has often been sensed. He died in 1989 and, ghost or not, I think the affable Irishman would like to know his presence is still felt there.

FELBRIGG HALL
The Man who Loved Books

The Felbrigg Hall we all know and love as a well-visited National Trust property today was built by John Windham for his son Thomas during the 17th century. The property

William Windham (1750–1810), a man who loved books. It is said his ghost returns to the library and still enjoys a quiet read by the flickering light of a phantom fire.

passed down the family line until William Windham III (1750–1810) inherited the house and estate in the late 18th century. William was a Tory and acted as Secretary for War (1794–1801); he later became a Whig. He will be best remembered in this county, however, as a bibliophile. He adored books and his magnificent library is preserved at the hall. But sadly it was also by a cruel twist of fate that books were to hasten his death.

When the library at the house of one of William's friends in London caught fire, he hastened to assist in evacuating the collection. He went back for just one more lot and some timbers collapsed upon him, causing an injury he bore with fortitude for over a year until 1810 when he died after an operation attempting to alleviate his pain. Poor William never got to look at all his books in full retirement and leisure – at least, not in this life.

In the 19th century, the antiquarian and author, Augustus Hare, recorded that he was told upon a visit to the hall that 'Mr Windham comes every night to look after his favourite books in the library. He goes straight to the shelves where they are; we hear him moving the table and chairs about.' Among the books he most highly treasured were those given to him by his friend, Dr Johnson, including the great man's personal, cherished copies of the *Iliad*, the *Odyssey* and the *New Testament*. It is said that when this specific combination of books is laid out in the library the ghost is most likely to appear, but he does not like crowds. I was told by a member of staff that he has been seen 'quite recently'. You might be lucky enough to glimpse him when all the visitors have gone home and it's dark outside. At times like these his ghost appears and sits snuggled up in his library chair to look at his beloved volumes, lit by the gentle glow of a ghostly fire in the grate. If there is any noise or hint that someone is near he just fades away.

Happisburgh
The Headless Smuggler

In the early 19th century Happisburgh was a small fishing village nestling cheek by jowl with the sea on the north-east coast of Norfolk. The village was also notorious for another business – smuggling. All could benefit if they helped the smugglers; lace, silk, baccy, tea and spirits could be yours – all duty free – but if you crossed the smugglers or, worse, informed on them to the Customs men merciless retribution would be your reward (see also the story of the coastguardman on the Bacton to Mundesley coastal path).

So when a glowing light was observed gliding silently between Cart Gap and Well Corner in Happisburgh folks simply 'watched the wall' and expected the gentlemen to ride by, although no horses or carts were heard. One night a group of farm labourers were returning home when they observed a glowing 'form' coming up the road from Cart Gap. As the light approached, more of the details of the object could be discerned. To their horror it was what appeared to be a headless body, which was noted to be carrying a bundle and to be missing its legs. Before the figure got too close the labourers fled in terror.

Two of the men were intrigued and brave enough to try to see the apparition again. On several nights they waited to no avail until about a week later when their vigil was rewarded and they hid in the hedge until the phantom passed them. These men could see that the ghostly smuggler also wore a leather belt with a huge buckle, and a pistol tucked into it. They also discovered that the ghost had not been decapitated but – rather like some hideous knapsack – the head was still attached. Subject to a crude hacking it was still hanging by a single strip of skin between the shoulders of the ghost, with its black beard and pigtail of hair almost

The great tower and sea mark that is Happisburgh church.

The famous coastline sentinel, Happisburgh Lighthouse.

touching the ground. Despite its dangling head the spirit glided along an unfaltering course. The labourers bravely followed the apparition along the road to Well Corner where it dropped its bundle into the well and then itself seemed to disappear over the side.

The farmers told their story to the village council and an investigation of the well was seen as the best way forward. Ropes and ladders were acquired for the purpose, then a candle stuck in a ball of clay was fixed to a rope and lowered down the well shaft to test the atmosphere. All seemed suitable for a human descent and a volunteer, a butcher's lad named Harmer, was sent down the forty-odd feet of the well with a lantern, sitting in a looped knot at the bottom of the rope. Initially he drew a blank but as he was being hauled up he spotted a piece of blue cloth hanging on a projecting brick. When this was brought up to the surface for examination, it was thought worthwhile to send the boy down again, this time armed with a long clothes prop. After a while in the depths the boy called up, 'I can feel something at the bottom.' An iron hake (pot hook) tied to a clothes line was lowered to him and the boy succeeded in hooking it onto the 'something' at the bottom of the well.

The boy was hauled up and the heavy mass on the bottom of the clothes line followed him to the surface soon after. Eagerly opened by those at the well-head, when the sodden wrappings were peeled away a pair of seaman's leather thigh boots was revealed – with the legs still inside!

The young lad Harmer had clearly been shaken by the experience and would not go down the well again. So a fisherman – filled with plenty of Dutch courage – was lowered down the well to investigate further. Keenly observed from above, the fisherman grappled around with the line and hake for a long time with no result. He could feel a lump but could not get the hook to connect with it. After a refresher of rum and water he set about his grim

Well Corner, later known as Pump Corner or Hill, Happisburgh.
Pictured c1910 when the pump was still in use: see far right of the photo.

task again and eventually 'caught' the object and they were both hauled to the surface. In this bundle was the body of the unfortunate seaman, his wounds corresponding exactly with the spectre seen by the locals.

Investigation of the known smugglers' 'runs' soon revealed signs of a mortal struggle. An area of blood-spattered ground and a large pool of congealed blood were discovered near Cart Gap, and a pistol that matched the one on the body was found driven into the dirt of an old and desolate bullock shed. It seemed that for some reason the smugglers had disagreed, perhaps over the division of spoils, or maybe someone had opened their mouth to the wrong person or turned informer. At the scene a few coins were found trodden into the dirt along with some smashed Schiedam bottles and these made the locals think that the smuggler and his killer or killers were probably Dutch. But who the murdered smuggler was or who killed him or why was never ascertained.

The well itself was capped, the ghost was silenced and a new pump, which saw the place name changed to Pump Corner, provided water for many generations afterwards. But now that the pump has been removed and the well filled in, the spirit of the Happisburgh smuggler seems to have been released again. On dark winter nights, when the winds threaten a gale, it is said that the hideous moans and wails of the spectral smuggler are still heard in the vicinity of the old well and a glowing form has been seen between Cart Gap and Pump Corner. A few local folks will confide that they believe they have seen the spectre in recent years but it seems the figure can no longer be seen at close quarters. Now it appears just as a floating, dimly-lit mass that flickers along the hedgerow – maybe the Happisburgh smuggler is still hunting for his killers …

MANNINGTON HALL
A Companion in the Library

The notable antiquarian Dr Augustus Jessop was a guest of the Right Hon Horatio Walpole, 4th Earl of Orford, at the 15th century Mannington Hall, two miles north-east of Saxthorpe. The purpose of his visit on 10th October 1879 was to consult some rare volumes that he had discovered were held in the library there.

Welcomed by his lordship, Dr Jessop spent a pleasant evening at dinner and playing cards but when the gathering broke up and everyone else went to bed the antiquarian could not resist a quiet time with the books he had come to see. He took six volumes

Mannington Hall, scene of a most remarkable encounter with a ghost.

down from the shelf and, placing them in a little pile at his right hand, settled himself at a table with the fire on his left, his work lit by four well-charged silver candlesticks. After some time, feeling a little chilly, Jessop 'knocked the fire together' and stood up to warm his feet. Shortly before 1 am the good doctor was very pleased with his progress and was confident he would have completed his task in another hour and would be in bed by 2 am. He got up, wound his watch, opened a bottle of seltzer water and settled down to work on the final treasured volume.

Dr Jessop's account of what happened next was published in the *Athenaeum* in January 1880 and is told here in his own words: 'I had been engaged upon it about half an hour and was just beginning to think that my work was drawing to a close, when, as

I was actually writing, I saw a large white hand within a foot of my elbow. Turning my head, there sat a figure of a somewhat big man, with his back to the fire, bending slightly over the table, and apparently examining the pile of books I had been engaged upon. The man's face was turned away from me, but I saw his closely cut reddish brown hair, his ear and shaved cheek, the eyebrow, the corner of the right eye, the side of the forehead and the large high cheek bone … He was dressed in what I can only describe as a kind of ecclesiastical habit of corded silk, close up to the throat, with a narrow rim of edging of about an inch of broad satin or velvet serving as a stand-up white collar and fitting close to the chin. The right hand, which had first attracted my attention, was clasping without any great pressure, the left hand; both hands were in perfect repose, and the large blue veins of the right hand were very conspicuous … I looked at my visitor for some seconds, and was perfectly sure he was not a reality.'

There sat Dr Jessop, a thousand thoughts running through his mind, alongside his spectral companion, so still and calm. Jessop continues, 'There he sat, and I was fascinated – afraid not of his staying, but lest he should go. Stopping in my writing I lifted my left hand from the paper, stretched it out to the pile of books, and moved the top one. I cannot explain why I did this – my arm passed in front of the figure and it vanished. I was simply disappointed, and nothing more. I went on with my writing as if nothing had happened, perhaps for another five minutes, and had actually got to the last few words of what I had determined to extract, when the figure appeared again, exactly in the same place and attitude as before. I saw the hands close to my own; I turned my head again to examine him more closely, and I was framing a sentence to address him, when I discovered that I dare not speak, I was afraid of the sound of my own voice. There he sat, and there sat I. I turned my head again to my work, and finished writing the two or three words I still had to write … Having finished my task,

I shut the book and threw it on the table. It made a slight noise as it fell and the figure vanished. Throwing myself back in my chair I sat for some seconds looking at the fire with a curious mixture of feeling, and I remember wondering whether my friend would come again, and, if he did, whether he would hide the fire from me.'

Jessop began to wonder if he would lose his nerve and replaced five of the six volumes. The sixth he brought back, laying it on the table in the same place as when he had first seen the spirit – and lo the spirit appeared again. Jessop concludes, 'By this time I had lost all sense of uneasiness. I blew out all the candles and marched off to bed, where I slept the sleep of the just – or the guilty – I know not which, but I slept very soundly.' But try as he might he could never explain who or what had shared the library with him late that night at Mannington Hall.

Before we depart from Mannington we must recall a far more frequently seen spectre, that of the White Lady in the old churchyard. The second Lord Orford had destroyed the tombs of the previous owners of the hall, the Scalmers, and she haunts the area looking for her final resting place. To placate this spirit, right up to the end of the 19th century the hearse containing each subsequent earl had to drive three times around the church before the body was interred.

North Norfolk Coast
Black Shuck – Devil Dog

One of the most ancient tales found along the Norfolk coast is that of the great, shaggy, black devil dog known by a variety of names – Old Shuck, the Shuck Dog and, the most popular, Black Shuck. Alleged sightings and spectral activities ascribed to Shuck are particularly prevalent in the area

The Salthouse Marshes – perhaps a haunt of Black Shuck.

between Weybourne and Overstrand, notably Shuck's Lane between Beeston and Overstrand, along which the great black dog is supposed to lope in twilight and through the hours of darkness. Said to date back centuries it has been suggested that 'Shuck' is derived from the Saxon word *Scucca*, meaning Devil; others suggest, bearing in mind our county's Viking past, a Scandinavian origin, with overtones of the cult of the hound of Odin. Perhaps the dog is a 'lost deity' or demon of the ancients who, no longer receiving his supplication and veneration, now seeks to claim souls in retribution.

Another account of the beast handed down by generations of North Norfolk fishermen tells of a tall-masted trading vessel foundering during a howling storm in the dangerous waters off Cromer in the early 18th century. Turning landwards, the ship ended up grounded at Salthouse where the furious waves caused it to begin to break up. The crew made a desperate bid to get ashore and chanced diving into the boiling waves and swimming to land. All were lost and the bodies of the captain and his wolfhound were discovered among the smashed wreckage washed up on the beach the following day. The jaws of the huge dog were still fastened to the captain's reefer jacket, the captain's dead hand continuing to grip the collar of his dog in a mute testimony to their loyalty in their final struggle against the waves. The dog was unceremoniously buried on the beach and the captain laid to rest in an unmarked grave in the churchyard. Reports of a strange spectral hound soon began to be recorded in the area and before the winter was over there were more storms – but what was that sound above the crashing waves? Was it the wind howling or, instead, the unquiet spirit of the wolfhound baying for his master?

The phenomenon of a black Devil, or demon, dog is far from unique to this coastline. Such beasts, known by different names, can be found all over the country. In Lancashire he is known as a Trash or Shriker; on the Isle of Man, the Mauthe or Moddey Dhoo; in Wales he is the Gwyllgi; Gurt Dog in Somerset; in coastal Suffolk the Galleytrot; and in Yorkshire he's the Padfoot. There was even the 'Black Dog of Newgate', said to have been seen around the walls of London's most notorious prison. Each beast has been described as ranging from the size of a calf up to that of a donkey. Most pant very audibly, if you dare or are unfortunate enough to get close, and are noted for fierce slavering jaws filled with sharp teeth. When the beast has passed or disappears, the smell of brimstone fills the air and lingers; scorch marks have also been recorded. Some tales, particularly from the notorious 'runs' of Shuck around the Cromer area, state that the beast is headless, but he still has a single eye, blazing like a coal from hell itself, floating where his head should have been. It was said that anyone seeing this beast would have a member of his or her family (or indeed themselves) go mad or die within the year. Another variant tells of an antidote – if you hold your tongue and do not tell anyone what you saw for a whole year, the evil curse of the Devil dog will be removed from you and your family.

While there is undoubted antiquity to the story of Black Shuck the accounts of his appearance had a resurgence in the 18th and 19th centuries when the tale fitted the uses of smugglers who operated all along the Norfolk coast. They would send ahead of their wagon train of contraband a pony disguised with a tattered black cloth thrown over it and a 'dark lanthorn' tied about its neck. Knowing the tale and fearing the fate of any who saw the Devil dog, few locals would hang about in the country lanes, to see close up if the lumbering form with one eerie glowing eye was subterfuge or the real phantom beast! (For similar scaremongering, see the ghastly apparition of Anne Boleyn's carriage, page 18.) One tale from a dark wintertime in the 19th century recorded in *Eastern Counties Collectanea* (1875) tells of a mischievous farmer who waylaid some of his friends near Cromer. He knew they would be walking up a lane near his land after dark so he tied a lantern to the head of a large ram and, attaching a long chain which dragged and clanked after it, he let it loose through a gap in a hedge to chase them up the road. His friends' reactions are not recorded.

Shuck has been spotted right along the Norfolk coast and also in Broadland areas. He manifests in his headless form to cross over Coltishall Bridge at the stroke of midnight and along Neatishead Lane where John Glyde jnr recounts in *Norfolk Garland* (1872): 'A person named Finch was walking in the road after dark and saw a dog … which snapped and snarled at him several times.' When he kicked out at the beast 'his foot went through him as through a sheet of paper'. At Salhouse 'a gigantic dog with a blazing eye in his forehead' was said to walk abroad after dark. When a young man and his brothers went out armed with sticks to search for the beast in the mid-19th century it was recorded that 'the people of the village thought they were going to certain death'.

Without doubt, Black Shuck was brought to the attention of Sir Arthur Conan Doyle, the creator of Sherlock Holmes, when he decided to take some of our healthy North Norfolk air in 1901 while recuperating from the enteric fever he contracted while reporting on the South African War. During his stay he travelled and played golf with his friend Bertram Fletcher Robinson, who was a collector of local tales, folklore and ghost stories. Conan Doyle heard the tale of the Devil dog and it was one of the main influences on his creation of the most famous case for his great detective – *The Hound of the Baskervilles*. Conan Doyle also visited Cromer Hall, a gothic building that, it must be said, bears a remarkable likeness to his description of Baskerville Hall in the novel.

When Christopher Marlowe, author of *People & Places in Marshland* (1927), came to the Wells area in the 1920s to investigate the phenomenon, he was chased by Shuck on Stiffkey Marshes. Huge phantom dogs have been seen over the last 150 years at Old Hunstanton, Salthouse Marshes and in Wells where a man was said to have been actually attacked. In more recent years, however, sightings of the classic, headless Black Shuck have been sparse. During the latter years of the Second World War a great dog was spotted at Thurton where it lumbered along behind a man on his bicycle and eventually disappeared through a solid wall. In November 1945 John Harries, the author of *The Ghost Hunter's Road Book* (1968), was stationed at RAF Swanton Morley and was also followed one night by a large and ominous dog which seemed to lope along silently, keeping up with him effortlessly as he cycled from his base to nearby East Dereham. In the summer of 1996 a family staying at Hemsby were walking back to their caravan park around midnight when their 19-year-old daughter witnessed a large dog with glowing red eyes, growling 'unlike any dog ... ever heard before'. Did this manifestation bring a curse with it? The family have certainly reported a run of bad luck ever since.

Most modern Shuck cases do not involve actual sightings but several instances have been reported of a dog, or similar beast, being heard snuffling and panting around coastal campsites, especially by those camping in tents. The creature is never claimed to brush against the wall of the tent; instead the feet of a heavy dog have been heard running around the field with such freedom and thundering speed that it seems as if no tents were pitched there. Those brave enough to investigate have seen nothing and no trace of a paw print has been discerned.

Over the border into Suffolk, at Walberswick in the 1940s a couple had rented a flat-topped hut and suffered a nightmarish night as some spectral animal threw itself against the walls. They barricaded the door and feared for their lives. The sound petered away with the dawn and no evidence of the attack was found on the walls or on the ground outside the hut. I mention this case because of its similarity to an incident recounted to me personally, and in confidence, by those directly involved in it. I met them socially rather than at one of my talks; they did not have a deep interest in ghosts. They were in fact sceptics but now, after this incident, have open minds. John and Anne Cator (their names have been changed for publication) were staying in a caravan at a coastal site near Cromer in the late 1980s. They were woken one night with a terrified start, as some 'heavy living lump' seemed to have thrown itself against the side of their caravan. As John was about to go and investigate, the heavy breathing of an animal was heard outside. It seemed as if the creature was circling the caravan, but as Anne pointed out the sound of the animal's panting was also eerily inside the caravan. Both John and Anne freely admit they were petrified. It was at a time when the story of the Surrey puma had recently been in the news and they wondered if this, too, was some wild animal that had escaped from a wildlife park or private collection. They dared not go outside until the sounds died away, and this did not happen until daylight broke. As they cautiously opened their caravan door and went out into the cool air of an early summer morning, the dew was heavy on the grass. Some areas still had traces of mud from the previous week's rainy weather, but there was no dent in the caravan where whatever it was had hit it with such ferocity and there was certainly no trace of a scratch, paw mark or track anywhere. Carefully phrased questions to their neighbours in their caravans revealed that those on either side had had undisturbed nights. They both wondered if they had shared the same dream – although they doubt that such a thing is possible.

A final thought to ponder is that as the sightings of black dogs decline reports of mysterious big cats, such as the Surrey puma, are on the increase across Great Britain. Perhaps our ancestors would not have recognised such a beast as a puma and thought it to be some large, vicious dog and undoubtedly a creation sent by the Devil himself ...

NORTH WALSHAM
The Fair Penitent

All of us who have been involved with amateur or professional dramatics, either as audience or cast, have encountered many wonderful people – but also certain ladies who, I must be careful here, are in the prime of life rather than the first flower of youth. Because of long years of loyal service, seniority in the company and their undoubted acting ability, these actresses often insist on playing the role of young heroines. Well, this is a cautionary tale for all ladies who may demand such roles ... or is there more to it?

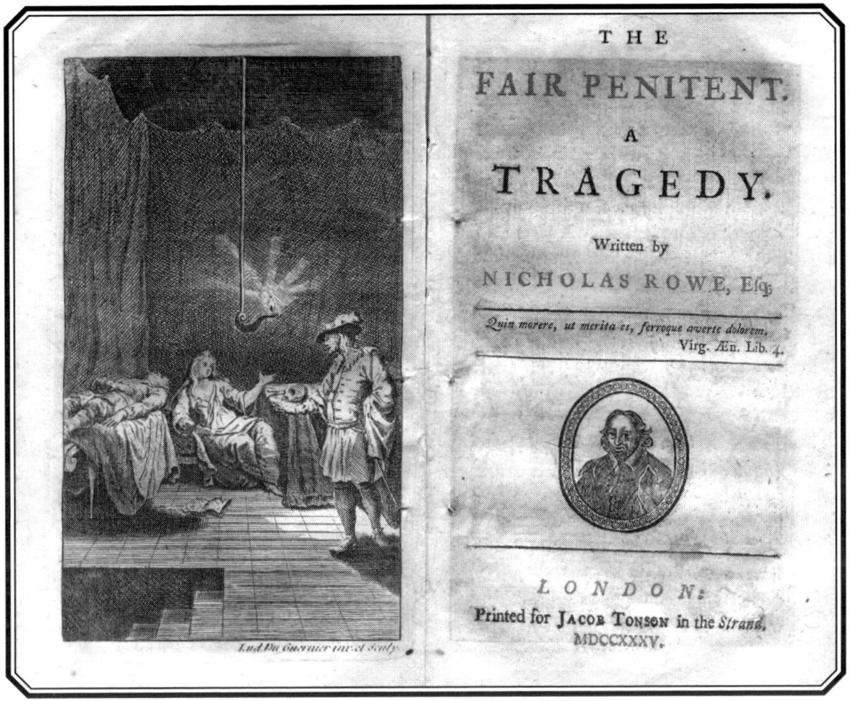

The title page and frontispiece from an 18th century edition
of The Fair Penitent *by Nicholas Rowe.*

In the flower of her youth, Mrs Barry was acclaimed for her performances on the London stage. When only in her teens, she played the female lead of Calista, the daughter of Sciolto, a nobleman of Genoa in Nicholas Rowe's *The Fair Penitent*, at Covent Garden (a role made famous by Elizabeth Barry, her famous predecessor). In the closing months of 1788 *The Fair Penitent* was due for a revival on the Norfolk theatre circuit. Although by this time Mrs Barry had been 'out to pasture', living in the theatrically christened Hamlet House on Bacton Road, North Walsham, for a number of years, she insisted on reviving her role of the 'young' female lead.

The opening night performance was staged at Mrs Barry's local theatre on Vicarage Street in North Walsham (nowadays a kitchen and home centre). This building had been an old barn and store converted for the purpose by entrepreneur, promoter and entertainer Billy Scragg. A few years later the theatre was considerably refurbished and almost completely rebuilt by the famous Fisher family who had a well-respected chain of theatres and their own theatre circuit in Norfolk. (In some later accounts of this story the following events have been erroneously described as taking place in Fisher's Theatre.)

Now, back to our opening night. All had gone well in the performance up to the final scene in the fifth act where our heroine, played by Mrs Barry, was bitterly bemoaning the death of Lothario (yes, *the* Lothario). The scene is set in an eerily lit charnel house, described thus: 'A room is hung with Black; on one side Lothario's body on a bier; on the other, a Table, with a Scull and other Bones and a Book and a Lamp on it.'

The opening song of the scene, reproduced here in full for the first time for over 100 years, was curiously prophetic of what happened next.

Hear, you Midnight Phantoms hear,
You who pale and wan appear,
And fill the wretch, who wakes with Fear.
You who wander, scream and groan,
Round the mansions once your own,
You, who still your crimes upbraid,
You, who rest not with the Dead;
From the Coverts where you stray,
Where you lurk, and shun the day,

From the Charnel and the Tomb,
Hither hast ye, hither come.

Chide Calista for delay,
Tell her 'tis for her, you stay;
Bid her die and come away.
See the Sexton with his Spade,
See the grave already made;
Listen, Fair one, to thy knell,
This music is thy passing Bell.

The scene reveals Calista, dressed all in black, her hair hanging loose and disordered. After the music and song she rises and comes forward. Outside the theatre, the night was certainly black and a storm of thunder and lightning heightened the atmosphere of the scene inside to unprecedented levels of intensity. Calista placed her hand upon the skull, and at that very moment she let out a piercing scream and reeled back in absolute horror. Almost simultaneously there was one almighty crack of thunder and lightning illuminated the whole theatre, bathing the room in a ghostly flash of bluish white light. In that flash of ghostly illumination the whole audience saw Mrs Barry collapse to the floor, but this was not part of the act. Fellow actors and stage staff rushed to the stricken actress, her eyes staring out like marbles, her face deathly ashen, and struck mute by some terrible shock. That night the show did *not* go on and the horrified audience left the building.

Mrs Barry was taken home to her bedchamber and attended by her loving husband and a local physician, but all to no avail and she died a few days later. Her hair allegedly turned white in this time and she never recovered complete composure. She did, however, utter a few garbled words about her husband and about the skull being deliberately placed there. Investigations were made into how the skull had been obtained and it was discovered that

Flaxman, the local sexton, had been asked to provide the theatre with one for the performance and had dug it up especially.

It transpired that the skull had belonged to one John Norris – Mrs Barry's first husband! And she had recognised it by the shard of metal embedded in its cranium. But there are two stories to explain why she was so horrified. Both tell of how Norris was a drunkard. The first states he was a river pilot in the Americas when he was attacked by brigands, one of whom crashed a rusty old cutlass onto the top of his skull. The blow did not kill him and he did recover from his wound but one shard of metal had been left in his head. Its removal would have killed him so it remained there until he died.

The other story has a more sinister edge and tells of how Mrs Barry had grown to hate her bullying drunkard of a husband and on one occasion had fought him off with a piece of wood which, unbeknownst to her, had a large nail embedded in it. This pierced Norris's skull and felled him like a pole-axed bullock. Flaxman had been bribed to bury the heavily wrapped body secretly in a quiet corner of the churchyard. Over the years this had weighed heavily on the sexton's mind and he was determined to clear his conscience by confronting Mrs Barry with the damning skull. In a final twist to the tale, another account says that Mrs Barry had confessed to the crime the instant it happened and had faced a formal hearing about the incident. Her story of self-defence had been believed and she was released under her own recognisance. Flaxman, for his own unrecorded reasons, disagreed with the verdict and thought he would cause her to be confronted by the skull on the dim, lamplit stage.

Whichever story you believe, the shock killed Mrs Barry and it was said that Hamlet House was never the same again. It never seemed to be occupied consistently by any one family after the death of the actress. Malevolent atmospheres, a sense of being watched and instances of bitterly cold spots were experienced all over the house. There were even reported sightings of 'a woman in white' flitting around the rooms and even being seen standing mournfully looking out of a window when the house was vacated. By the late 1960s Hamlet House was in a very dilapidated state and it was around that time it finally burnt down in a mysterious fire. When the flames were licking out of the windows several onlookers saw a 'white figure' at one of the windows and even a fireman though he saw 'something' inside. No body or hint of human remains was found in the charred remains of the house.

Today, Hamlet House has been demolished and the whole site converted to the houses of Hamlet Close. But the story of the ghost of Hamlet House did not end with the destruction of the building. Throughout the 1970s and up to the present day residents, and even visitors who have no idea of the house's history, have had fleeting glimpses of the shade of a woman with long hair. She wears a long white flowing gown and floats across gardens and straight through fences. A number of people living in the close have reported to me that they have heard very repetitive murmurings 'almost as if someone was rehearsing lines for a play', heard from 'just over the fence' or along the hedge line, when they knew no-one was there. In some of the houses there have been instances where electrical appliances appear to 'short out' for no reason or lights have been discovered mysteriously turned on in empty rooms. One couple whose neighbours were away on holiday were so concerned about the voices that they went around to investigate and found nobody there – even the garden gate was padlocked.

Perhaps, the last word should be taken from the Epilogue of *The Fair Penitent* itself:

You could see the tripping Dame could find no favour,
Dearly she paid for Breach of good Behaviour,
Nor could her Loving Husband's Fondness save her.

SALTHOUSE HEATH AND CLEY
The Snowy Comrade

In the early 19th century Norfolk was subjected to a number of extremely severe winters. At the time of the following events in 1814 the temperature had fallen 20 degrees below freezing point and the rivers between Norwich and Great Yarmouth were rendered unnavigable. The roads were little better. Carriers who had arrived in Norwich in the light snow of the early morning found that the roads became blocked by the evening and even the Royal Mail had to be brought to Norwich on single horses. Snowdrifts were high and most of the North Norfolk coastal roads were impassable.

In spite of the conditions, one very determined sailor who had just been paid off from his ship at Great Yarmouth resolved to return home to his family, who lived in a small cottage in Cley. He hitched a lift on a couple of carrier's carts, slept one night in a hay barn, and on the second day of his journey, was lucky to get a ride to Kelling from a kindly farm worker with his wagon. However, they could not negotiate the road to Cley because of the severe snowdrifts. The farm wagon had to turn back but, undaunted, the sailor swung his kitbag over his shoulder, wound his scarf around his head, pulled his hat down firmly against the wind, drew his coat closer around him to shrug off the cold, and set off to walk home.

The going was not too bad as he trudged through the snow across the fields and along the familiar lanes he knew from his childhood, but as he began to go over Salthouse Heath the gently falling snow grew more and more intense until it became a real blizzard, so thick that he could no longer discern any familiar landmarks. It was then that he espied an old man making his way through the swirling snow ahead of him. The sailor realised that

The view across the rolling countryside to Cley church.

the old man could not be far from his home in such foul weather; perhaps he could give directions or at least offer some shelter until the storm abated.

The young man leapt through the drifting snow and called out, but it was only when he drew level that he got a reaction. The old man stopped, turned to face the sailor and regarded him for a moment, his eyes twinkling and a smile turning up the corners of his mouth under his big white beard. As the sailor went to speak the old man raised a gloved finger to his whiskered lips, looked skyward and then prodded his finger to the heavens likewise. He then turned his heavily swathed form back to the direction he was travelling and, pointing forward, bade the sailor follow. Despite the lack of any verbal communication the young man got the distinct impression that he was being advised to keep his head up. With little other option and the snow closing in, the sailor lifted his chin and carried on through the snow with his new companion.

As the light began to fail the blizzard died down. Eventually, the old man turned up a cart track and indicated his cottage with a sweep of his arm. Lamps illuminated the windows and smoke whirling out of the chimney made the sailor long even more to get home. He soon recognised the familiar landmark of Wiveton church, then Blakeney high on the hill in the distance, and finally Cley, in the bowl of the valley. He knew he was not far from home now and made it to his cottage door and the embrace of his family as darkness drew in.

The following morning the storm had abated and the sailor thought he would like to take some small token of thanks to the old man who had helped him. Slipping two fine flasks of rum he had hidden from the Excise into his coat (one for the old man and another for himself on his cold journey) he set out across the white fields to find the cottage. Sure enough there it was, the lights glowing and the chimney smoking. Stomping up the cart track the sailor knocked at the door. A little old lady, even more wizened than the old man he had met, opened it. The sailor enquired if her husband was in and explained how he wished to thank him for his kindness. The old lady's eyes filled with tears as she told him that her husband had been dead for over ten years. Thinking there must be some mistake, the sailor described the man, beard and all. The poor lady was beside herself; it was just as her late husband looked and just how he was dressed when they found him during the last great snowstorm when he lost his way and perished on Salthouse Heath.

Taking his leave from the lady the sailor rushed down the path and onto the heath. Despite there being more snow he could still discern his tracks from the night before, but that was what really made the young man shudder – there was only one set of footprints!

SWAFIELD AND BACTON WOOD
Bloody Will Suffolk

William Suffolk was born and bred in the hamlet of Swafield near North Walsham. In 1797 he was 46 years old, a married man who worked hard on the family smallholding to support his wife, his four children and his long-widowed father. All seemed well in this typical country family until Will's wily eye rested on their attractive young neighbour, Mary Beck.

Their relationship resulted in Mary falling pregnant. Her state was kept a secret as long as they could but when her corsets and skirts would no longer conceal the ever-growing bump they fled to 'the grass countries' where she gave birth to the child in secret. Neither seemed to want the poor babe and Suffolk was 'confederate' in the child's murder and disposal of the body.

Now, whether Mrs Suffolk was aware of the situation and took the old scallywag back after he pleaded forgiveness or whether Suffolk managed to concoct some story to cover his absence with young Mary is not clearly recorded, but it seems that both parties returned to their respective households after their absence. They had one last fling after their return but Mary had made up her mind she wanted no more of their affair.

Suffolk caught up with Mary the following day near Bacton Heath when she was returning home after selling three bushels of

THE
LAST DYING
Speech and Confession,
OF
William Suffolk,

Who was executed this Day on the CASTLE-HILL, Norwich: For the most cruel and barberous Murder of MARY BECK, (who is to be hung in Chains near where the Murder was done.)

I WILLIAM SUFFOLK am in the forty-six year of my age, was born in the parish of Sweael, in the County of Norfolk, of poor but honest parents, following the employ of husbandry, till this unhappy thing took place. Accordingly I became acquainted with Mary Beck, and having gone up and down the grass countries for some years we cohabited together as man and wife; she living near to me, we secretly carried on the wicked correspondence together as we had done before, during which time she fell with child by me, tho' unknown to the public; after this we went into the grass countries again, where she was delivered of her infant child, which I confess as a dying man, that she and I was both confederate in the murder of the infant, tho' unknown to the world; therefore as a dying man I confess the justice of my sentence being guilty of the murder.

She having sold three bushels of wheat, upon the return, I requested the money which she refused to give me, telling me it was not her property to give, for she owed' it to her brother: I then ask her why she yield'd to me the night past, she said she would not yield to me no more, nor be no more in my company. I then stroke her a blow with a cudgel I had in my hand, upon which she fell to the ground; I than repeated the blows three times, and left her for dead for what I know: I then took and dragged her cross the horse-road, and left her head in the cart-rutt, supposing the people would think she was kill'd by accident; but herein sin and the devil deceived me, for no sooner had I done it than I was forc'd to confess of the murder: But being harden'd in sin I told the Justice if I got acquitted of this, I had two more to murder, and that was my Wife and the Brother of the deceased, but here I hope they will freely forgive me. My Mother has been dead a long time, but I have a poor aged Father now alive, a Wife and four poor little children; herein I earnestly beg that all good people would not cast any reflection on them for my conduct. I die in peace with all mankind. Witness my Hand
William Suffolk.

The awfull reflection on the horrid crime of murder, first murder committed with premeditated design is in general the last stage of a long course of wickedness, during which the villain is hardened by constant practices, to such a degree as to stop at nothing to obtain his purposes what ever they are, men of this discription tho' they perhaps may commit murder, but once in their lives, it is not from a sence of its wickedness, for they are always capable of it, but from a dread of its consequences; so certain is the truth of the old saying murder cannot be hid, that, they knew that by committing this last and worst of crimes, that they would sum up their wickedness, and fill the measure of their iniquities: Secondly murder is frequantly the result of a suden impulse of passion, proceeding from provecation, murder committed under such circumstances is in generally considered as less wicked, and people are apt to think the murderer rather unfortunate than guilty; especialy it his former conduct of life has been without reproach, men that have so little guard over their passions, should for the assisting grace of God; otherwise they may some time commit a sin of the most henious kind, the punishment of which is certain and severe. To conclude murder is the greatest of crimes, as it render the perpetrator of it the abhorrence of his fellow creature, brings him unpitied to a shameful death, and above all draws down upon his guilty head the heavy displeasure of Almighty God. Let us pray therefore least we fall into temptation, either from dishonesty or passion, that may lead us to so dreadful a sin.

Broadside sold at the execution of William Suffolk in 1797.

wheat, the profits of which Suffolk considered were his. Mary indignantly said that the money was not hers to give but belonged to her brother. The argument soon escalated as Suffolk made advances towards Mary and she rebuffed him. He demanded to know why she had yielded to him the night before, to which she replied that she would yield no more and she did not wish to be in his company again. This was too much for Suffolk and he struck her a mighty blow with the cudgel he was carrying. It felled the girl whereupon he rained a further three massive blows upon her head with his stick, cracking her skull. He then dragged her lifeless body across the cart track and left her head in one of the ruts, stamping it to a hideous pulp for good measure in the hope that those who discovered her would believe she had been killed in some tragic accident.

On his way home Suffolk was spotted by a group of locals who challenged him as to why he was spattered in blood. Still in a rage, his answers did not add up. A cry arose shortly after with the discovery of poor Mary's body and the parish constable was summoned. Such was the arrogance of William Suffolk that when he was brought before the justice he stated that if he was acquitted of the murder of Mary 'I had two more to murder … my wife and Mary's brother.' Found guilty of the killing, Suffolk was executed on Castle Hill in Norwich, where he was hanged before a large crowd. The notoriety of 'Bloody Will Suffolk' and the whole sordid tale was recorded on broadsheets and in ballads and was even the subject of church sermons around the county – a salutary tale to warn of the dangers of illicit passions and what they would drive people to do in their pursuit.

The body of 'Bloody Will' was parboiled, tarred and placed in a cage. It was then carted back to near the scene of his abominable crime and mounted on a gibbet erected on the cart track just off the North Walsham to Bacton road. (Although nothing remains today of the gibbet Bloody Will was exhibited from, Gibbet Piece can still be found in Bacton Wood (OS Explorer 252: GR 312311). Many folks came to view the swinging remains of this notorious criminal until his body became so unsightly and depleted by souvenir hunters that it was taken down by order of the magistrates and buried without ceremony near the site in June 1803.

Ever since that time, local folklore has told of the creaking groans of the gallows and the rusty screech of the old gibbet cage. Low and tragic moans were still being heard above the sound of the trees on a windy night years after the gallows had been taken down. Some local people still don't like the area and find themselves 'getting the shivers' there at dusk, even on warm summer evenings. In the early 1980s some children who had no idea of the crime or burial were playing in the woods near the site when they came across a skeleton, lying in a mossy glade. Not daring to touch the horrific discovery they ran home and reported the matter to their parents who after a little persuasion came to investigate. Despite finding the exact spot, there was no trace of any remains. The children, however, swore by what they had seen. Could it be that the earthly remains of 'Bloody Will' still cannot rest in peace?

WALSINGHAM
The Misery in the Bridewell

In 2005 I was taking a group of my students around the old bridewell at Little Walsingham. Although it was autumn, the weather was clear and fine and we had all had an enjoyable visit to the nearby Shirehall Museum and proceeded to the bridewell in good spirits and in sunshine. Admittedly, many old buildings, churches, castles or ruins can have certain atmospheres about them. There is nothing paranormal about that; anyone with an imagination and a sense of history would probably feel some emotion or sense of atmosphere when exploring such places, especially for the first time. I have taken several groups around this fascinating and unrestored house of correction over the years and am aware that some students know they have problems with confined spaces and wish to wait outside. The trouble with this visit was that several of the group went inside and came straight out again feeling very cold and saying, 'I didn't like it in there.' Most of the group, however, carried on; we felt cold but were fine.

Over lunch one of the ladies who had come straight out talked to me confidentially. She said she had never felt anything quite like the atmosphere in the bridewell, which she could only describe as 'such misery'. Another lady told me that she had felt the cold 'pass through her'; she physically shivered and was, again, left with a sensation of 'intense misery'. I did not feel that these ladies were prone to flights of fancy, and they were obviously genuinely concerned about what they had felt in that building, particularly at the far end of the ground floor range of cells. I am certain they had not stayed in the building long enough to read the signs indicating that the area in question was the 'dark cell', which could be shuttered to leave it in inky blackness. In the 'dark cell', refractory prisoners would often be restrained and fed a wretched diet of bread and water as a punishment for any misdemeanours they might have committed while in the prison. And remember, the separate and silent system meant that this horrible punishment would have been suffered in solitary confinement and in silence – by order!

By the late 18th century bridewells, otherwise known as 'houses of correction', just like the one at Little Walsingham, could be found all over the country. In 1843 Walsingham Bridewell consisted of 53 cells, several day rooms, airing yards, an infirmary

Inside the Walsingham Bridewell, where the misery of its inmates lingers on.

and no less than 4 tread wheels used to power mill stones for grinding corn and so on. Mostly, those who were held in bridewells were petty criminals or those awaiting trial. This return from 1828 gives some indication of the sort of criminals held there: William Williamson – for refusing work, one calendar month to tread wheel; Matthew Edge – for disobeying an order of bastardy, three months; Samuel Lake – for leaving his wife chargeable to the parish of Bale, one calendar month to tread wheel; Catherine Watson – for misdemeanour, one calendar month hard labour; Thomas Smith, James Pigge and William Bullock – being found poaching in the night, two calendar months hard labour; John Chestney – for a misdemeanour, one month to tread wheel.

Several deaths would have occurred within the bridewell walls over the years and, without doubt, misery, despair, hatred, curses and violence would have permeated the stonework. Perhaps the atmospheres are residual energy from such concentrated emotions in an unrestored and unspoilt building. In this case it was not just a one-off; when researching this book I spoke to a photographer friend of mine who went with his long-term partner to photograph the bridewell. A well-balanced and intelligent lady, she too was greatly affected by the intensity of the sadness or atmosphere of sheer misery she experienced on the ground floor here.

I suggest there are one or two candidates in particular for this haunting, because it was to Walsingham that Frances 'Fanny' Billing and Catherine Frary, the notorious 'Burnham Poisoners', were removed and held pending the investigation of their crimes. Both were known to consort with witches at Burnham and Sall and especially with 'Mother' Hannah Shorten of Wells. On the afternoon of Fanny's arrest Catherine had asked Fanny's son Joseph to hire her a horse and gig to drive her to Sall; as Joseph recalled, 'to go to a woman who was something of a witch, that that woman might tie Mr Curtis's tongue [Mr Curtis was the keeper of the Walsingham bridewell] so that he might not question my mother'. But the truth came out and it was soon revealed that Billing and Frary had causing the excruciating deaths of both Robert Frary (husband of Catherine) and Mary Taylor, the wife of Peter Taylor (the man Fanny Billing was having an affair with), by administering arsenic in dumplings and gruel.

Once in the Walsingham bridewell, both women had deteriorated fast as they were interrogated and scorned as killers. The spirit and health of Catherine Frary were recorded in contemporary accounts as so 'broken' within the walls of the prison that concerns were raised at her ability to stand trial. Perhaps it is her misery and wickedness that, above all, lingers to haunt the old bridewell at Walsingham, although she did not end her days there. Both Billing and Frary were tried at the Norfolk Assizes in Norwich, found guilty of murder and both ended up being hanged 'by the neck until dead' upon the gallows at Norwich Castle in front of a vast crowd on Monday, 10th May 1835. Frary went to her end 'near collapse and had to be carried up the steps of the scaffold'. Placed upon the gallows trapdoor, and the ropes put around their necks, the two women held hands, the fatal bolt was drawn, the trap fell open and they were plunged into eternity.

WAXHAM
New Year's Eve with the Brograves

On 31st December 1733, New Year's Eve was celebrated by the Brograve family at their newly acquired country house, Waxham Hall, for the first time. Described by J. Wentworth Day as 'a bleakly beautiful manor house', only one wing remains of the once grand Mockbeggar's Hall, originally built in the early 12th century when it was said to be twelve miles inland. Today, the sea laps little more than 200 yards from its gatehouse.

Many stories have become attached to the rustic gentry family of Brograve, from the duels they fought to their pack of ferocious hounds, including the account of Sir 'Barney' Brograve who took a wager and mowed for his soul against the Devil himself. Sir Barney came off the winner after he had stuck iron rods amongst the corn the Devil was to mow, causing Old Nick to exclaim, 'Blas me Barney Bor, these bunks cut hard!' Some say the Devil has taken some of his dues back by biting away at the land of the Brograves through storm encroachments and erosion by the sea into their coastal estates. Although Barney died a bachelor it was said, with typical Victorian prudery, that 'he dotted the countryside with his portrait'.

For as long as the Brograves were at Waxham Hall, we are told that they would entertain their dead ancestors every New Year's Eve: Sir Ralph who was killed in the Crusades, Sir Edmund in the Barons' Wars, Sir John at Agincourt, Sir Frances in the Wars of the Roses, Sir Thomas at Marston Moor, Sir Charles at Ramillies. This motley crew would disappear with the chimes of midnight, not to be seen again until the next year.

WORSTEAD
The White Lady of St Mary's

Many a fireside around the Worstead area was graced by this tale, which has a definite *ring* of truth. A White Lady was believed to appear in the tower of St Mary's church as the clock struck midnight on Christmas Eve.

It was the custom at that time for the senior bellringer or the sexton to ring in Christmas Day for a few minutes on the bell as the clock's chimes subsided. On this particular evening in 1830 a group of locals had gathered in the nearby King's Head and, of course the subject turned to the White Lady. In fact, it was the usual custom of a small group from the inn to go over and witness the Christmas bellringing, but on this occasion one wag piped up that he was not afraid of any white lady and that he would go alone to ring the bell. He even boasted that if he saw her he would give her a kiss.

As his companions waited in the doorway of the inn, their friend, fired up with Dutch courage, strode off confidently into the darkness. They soon heard the church clock strike twelve but no Christmas bell rang. They waited, minute after minute, until five minutes had passed but no peal rang out so they grabbed lanterns and rushed across to the church. As they entered the west door all was quiet – as quiet as the grave. Rushing up the church tower to the bell chamber, they began to hear a disturbing gibbering. In the chamber they discovered their friend, who had pushed himself up into a corner in a crouching position, his limbs shaking, his eyes rolling, with the rest of him paralysed with fright. He soon lapsed into insensibility and was carefully lowered through the chamber trapdoor and carried to the inn. Restoratives administered, he only recovered enough to open his eyes and whisper, 'I've seen her! – There!! There!!' before he lapsed back into unconsciousness and died later that same day. I claim nothing more but add that the Worstead church burial register records one Green Potter, aged 65, who was buried in the churchyard on 3rd January 1831.

A postscript to this story may be found in 1975 when Diane Bertelot was visiting the church with her husband Peter and son David while they were up on holiday from Essex. Diane had recently been troubled by sickness and was feeling unwell. The church was empty and Peter snapped a photo of his wife while she was sitting on a bench a short distance from the font. They thought nothing more about it until they decided to have friends

St Mary's church, Worstead.

around for a slide show of their trip and someone noticed a figure behind Diane in this picture. Clear as day, it appears to be a woman dressed in a bonnet and a long white dress – but that was impossible, as nobody else had been in the church. When they returned to Worstead a year later they brought the photo and spoke to the local rector, who recalled the story of the White Lady, but he knew the figure as a healer. He said that the ghost had not been seen for many years, but when she did appear there was usually sickness about.

Could it be that poor old Green Potter was ill at the time the White Lady appeared to him but, instead of a cure, the fright killed him?

ACLE
The Telling Stain

On the outside of the stonework on the up-river side of the old Acle river bridges was a red splash said to be a bloodstain. It was so engrained into the stone that even when a portion of the stone was chipped away the mark was apparent again the next day. A number of tales have grown up to account for the stain over the years but one seems to be more convincing than the others. This version dates back about 350 years to the case of the local ne'er-do-well Josiah Burge, a big, ugly brute of a man whose behaviour had been violent since his childhood. He was said to have pushed one of his playmates, a 7-year-old boy, into the path of a horse and the lad was trampled to death.

Burge had no endearing features and his whole attitude and demeanour did not attract women. That said, he did, like many bullies, blackmail and intimidate a certain number of local cronies to join in, or turn a blind eye to, his nefarious deeds. Too mean to pay for any of the whores of Yarmouth – and a man they probably would have turned down if he had approached them – Burge determined to take a woman by force. On this fatal evening he lurked in the shadows not far from Acle Bridge and presently a young girl came by carrying a pot of warm soup to a sick relative. As she walked up the road she became aware of someone closing on her. She quickened her pace, but the feet behind her did the same and before she knew it the big, powerful man had knocked her into a ditch. The girl fought hard and managed to slip out of Burge's slavering embrace. Pulling up his breeches, Burge's fury knew no bounds. He chased after her and leapt on her again, raining blow after blow upon her with his powerful fists. In the process of the beating or hauling her down for that final time he broke her neck. Burge simply walked away and left her lying there like a discarded, bloody rag.

With no clear evidence and certainly no forensics Burge was never accused of the crime but many had their suspicions.

Some time after the murder, the girl's brother came back from military service abroad and, his identity unknown to Burge, he happened to overhear the drunken killer boast about the way he had killed the girl and got away with it. There were too many of Burge's cronies in the pub so the young man waited until the bully left. Burge was alone and still the worse for drink as he crossed Acle Bridge. As he leaned over the edge to be sick, the brother saw his chance and quickly whipped the blade of a knife around Burge's neck, cutting his throat from ear to ear. The blood poured down the bridge and as the body slumped to the floor the brother's anger drove him to plunge the blade into Burge's dying body many times.

Rather like Burge, he just walked away and no evidence was found to connect him to the crime. By some quirk of fate a year later, to the day – 7th April – the brother was crossing the bridge late at night when a huge skeleton leapt over the parapet, pressed him to the wall and slashed his throat from ear to ear. Locals assumed that the murder had been carried out by one of Burge's old cronies. Exactly a year later, however, a fresh pool of blood was found to well up on the bridge on the spot where Burge and the brother had been killed, and at midnight the skeleton of a once tall and broad man was said to have been seen. In one account, thought to date from 1828, the Earl of Vauxhall and guests were travelling over Acle Bridge when their coach came to an abrupt halt and the horses began to whinny. Looking outside, to his horror the Earl saw: 'A man standing at the corner of the bridge carelessly leaning against the wall, when suddenly before our very eyes a huge live skeleton, glowing with an uncanny light, sprung on him, forcing his head back on the parapet, and stabbing him all over. Lord Monty, our coachman Berris and I rushed forward to try and seize the murderer, but on arriving at the spot, not a soul was to be seen, but there was fresh blood all over the stone.'

HICKLING
The Drummer Boy

Another classic Norfolk ghost story, and one of my personal favourites, is that of the phantom drummer boy of Hickling Broad. The tale is set against the cold backdrop of winter 1813–14 after childhood friends Lilly Ducker and John Sadler were reunited when the young man, now a drummer in the Grenadiers, came home on leave. Soon their old friendship was renewed and they fell in love.

Now, Lilly lived with her family in the cottage that her father, Jesse, had as a marshman. He was a hard-working man and only wanted the best for all his children and he was none too keen to see one of his daughters 'gone for soldier'. But rather than risk trying to impose a ban, he thought it might be a good idea if the encounters of the young couple were to be at the river bank in future – one on each side. If they really did love one another no harm could come from such a test. What Jesse did not expect, however, was the severity of the frosts that winter, when the waters across Hickling Broad froze solid.

One night as Lilly waited to hear from John at a place near the water's edge called Swim Coots (OS Explorer OL40: GR 415212)

Dusk falls over Hickling Broad, just the time when you might hear the swish of ghostly skates and the roll of the drum of the drummer boy who drowned here.

she heard the swish of blades on the ice and a roll on the drum from her soldier boy as out of the gloom he came, skating to her arms. It was a romantic dream come true and neither wanted the assignations to stop, indeed John resolved to buy himself out of the army and settle down with Lilly. The plans they made saw them married and having children. Both were so happy. They could not bear to leave each other's arms and longed for the next evening's meeting.

On the fateful night of 24th February 1814 Lilly waited for her love by the bank as usual. She soon heard the roll of the drum and the merry whistle of John as he skated over the ice. There is no way of knowing whether the young drummer was aware that there had been a thaw and simply risked the journey for his love – or maybe there was a weak patch in the ice – but before he emerged from the gloom there was a horrible crack and a sickening splash followed by an unnatural silence.

It is unclear if the body of John Sadler was ever recovered from his watery grave but not long after this tragic event the strange figure of a uniformed drummer was spotted apparently skimming over the water of Hickling Broad during the half-light between afternoon and evening. He has not been seen for many years but his drum rolls and whistled tunes have been heard up to the present over the still air of the evening, especially during the month of February.

INGHAM
The Knightly Walk

An old tale associated with Ingham church concerns the two remarkable tombs of Sir Oliver de Ingham and Sir Roger de Bois. Both date from the 14th century and both knights are depicted life size and recumbent in their full armour. Sir Roger, who has his wife beside him, rests his head on the decapitated head of a defeated enemy. A typically fanciful tale embroidered around many a fireside tells of how on every 2nd August the two knights magically become flesh and, swinging their legs off their tombs, stiffly walk together out of the church down to Stalham Broad where they do combat with a figure of Middle-Eastern appearance. Once their enemy is slain the knights

The life-size figures of Sir Roger de Bois and his wife in Ingham church.

The recumbent armoured figure of Sir Oliver de Ingham.

dust themselves down and walk back to the church to rest for another year.

Dear Charles Sampson in *Ghosts of the Broads* said that he and a group of interested friends witnessed this phenomenon (he cites the anniversary appearance as 3rd June) and they even took photographs of the tombs with the knights absent. I have enjoyed the stories in his book all my life, and indeed several are recalled in this collection, but I must agree with Sampson himself: 'how much is actually true must be left to the reader's discretion'.

But we must not dismiss the ghosts of Ingham too quickly. Ernest Suffling in *The History & Legends of the Broad District* (1891) notes 'a transparent lady at Ingham ... seen, by those whose vision is acute enough, in the large gravel pit near the church'. In the early 1990s I frequented the nearby Swan Inn when it was kept by Keith Fiddy, a friend of our family. When he had the car park put in between the pub and the church and some building work carried out, the ancient skeleton of a woman was uncovered. The old religious building that had stood on the site centuries before was a Trinitarian priory dedicated to St Mary and the Holy Trinity. This was an all-male order but it was founded by Sir Miles Stapleton and Lady Joan, the daughter of Sir Oliver de Ingham who lies in the church. Perhaps she was the ghost who walked, disturbed after the priory she helped to found fell into ruins?

One night in the pub I was talking to a few of the locals, and rather than the tale of the two knights they told of the figure of an old man and his dog who had been spotted at night on the road between Ingham and Stalham. Apparently he seemed to walk in the middle of the road and a couple of car drivers had actually come to the pub to use the phone in a fearful state. Each time the story was just about the same: 'an old man had appeared out of nowhere and disappeared off the bonnet' before they could hammer on their brakes.

IRSTEAD, THURLTON AND THE NORFOLK BROADS
Hyter Sprites, Jack o' Lantern and Will o' the Wisp

It is an intriguing feature of the research of the ghosthunter that occasionally phenomena of a similar description will be ascribed to quite different causes. Good examples are the

Variously described as Hyter Sprites, Jack o'Lantern and Will o' the Wisp,
these mysterious 'lights' have appeared along the coast and especially
across Broadland and marshes for centuries.

ghostly balls of bluish light that sometimes appear to flicker and hover over graves or over Broadland, often in wet or 'murky' weather. They are known variously across the county as corpse lights or ghost lights in churchyards, hyter sprites, Jack o' Lanterns, Will o' the Wisps on the broads and shiners on the lakes and expanses of still water around Breckland (although some of the names seem to be applied generically). These strange lights are said by some to glide around churchyards and rest upon the graves of the recently interred; in other areas they are ascribed to the glowing spirits of people who lie uneasy in their graves. Others say they are watch lights placed there by certain kindly spirits to keep

The grave of Joseph Bexfield in Thurlton churchyard.

evil ones from burial grounds when the spirits of the good are vulnerable.

These lights or lanterns are certainly curious things. Several accounts state that, if the light appears in a field, say, and there was a man on each side, if one of them whistled the light would be drawn towards him. But such an action would be seen as foolish because the lights could cause harm and even chase unsuspecting passers-by. In *Eastern Counties Magazine* of 1900, Lady Cranworth, a remarkable folklorist, published an article that related just such a tale from a Cromer fisherman, who recounted: 'There's no saying what that will du to you, if that light on you! There was a young fellow coming home one evening and he see the Lantern Man coming for him and he run; and that run!' The young man took shelter in the house of old Giles and the old man thought he would try to draw the spirit. 'He got a candle and held that out of the window on the end of a pole. And fust he held that out right high; and the Lantern Man, he come for that and he come underneath it. And then he held that out right low and the Lantern Man he come up above it. And then he held that out right steady, and the Lantern Man come for that and he burst it all to pieces … But they du say, if the Lantern Man light upon you, the best thing is to throw yourself flat on your face and hold your breath.'

Some explain the strange lights away as insects, moths or even self-igniting natural gas, but whatever these strange lights may be, they do still occur. Those who know Broadland would never fail to advise people against attempting to walk across the marshes after dark, but the danger is always seen as far more acute when the Jack o' Lanterns are out. The hazard was well known to wherrymen, who had seen 'balls of flame' float across the marshes and cling to the mast of a wherry like St Elmo's Fire. In August 1809 38-year-old Joseph Bexfield, a wherryman who had known the marshes all his life, scoffed at the belief and stubbornly set out to cross the marsh to Thurlton Staithe when the Jack o' Lanterns were glowing all over the marshes. The older men called out 'Don't be led astray', but it was no good, Joe Bexfield was never seen alive again. His body was washed up between Reedham and Breydon and he lies buried on the north side of Thurlton church, north being the area of churchyards that was often used for the burial of strangers and those who died in mysterious circumstances.

In the Broadland village of Irstead in 1849 the Reverend John Gunn noted the story that local 'knowing woman' Mrs Lubbock told of the Jack o' Lantern. She recalled incidents from before the time of the local enclosures in 1810. The Irstead Jack o' Lantern was frequently seen when the nights were 'roky'. 'I have often seen it there,' she said, 'rising up and falling and twistering about and then up again. It looked exactly like a candle in a lantern.' The light seemed to prefer to appear at Heard's Holde in Alder Carr Fen Broad on the Neatishead side. The area was said to have been cursed after a man named Heard, who had been 'guilty of some unmentionable crimes', had drowned there. Mrs Lubbock continued, 'If any one were walking along the road with a lantern at the time he appeared, and did not put out the light immediately, Jack would come against it and dash it to pieces.' She also told of a gentleman who was riding in the adjoining parish of Horning one night when he mocked the light and the myth only to have the light fly at him and knock him off his horse. In *Norfolk Garland* (1872) it was recorded that after the spirit of Heard began to take more human form and started appearing at certain places he had frequented when alive, the Neatishead people wanted to discourage the spirit and end his mischief once and for all: 'Three gentlemen attempted to lay the ghost by reading verses of Scripture, but he always kept a verse ahead of them, and they could do nothing, till a boy brought a couple of pigeons and laid them down before him. He looked at them and lost his verse, and then they bound his spirit.'

St Benet's Abbey.

LUDHAM
The Abbot of St Benet's

A potent blend of legend and ghosts surrounds the ruins and site of St Benet's Abbey whose few remaining walls and gatehouse look so lonely out there on the marshes near Ludham (OS Explorer OL40: GR 380158). In its heyday the abbey of St Benet-at-Holme had great power in Norfolk and wealth from the lands and tithes it held in many parishes across the county. It was founded before the Norman Conquest, and an old legend recounts how, when the Conqueror's men came to claim the abbey, they were turned away and forced to lay siege, but the Abbot's man who carried the messages of negotiation to and from the soldiers outside was bribed. The deal was that if he opened the great gate of the abbey after dark to let the soldiers in, they, in return, would make him Abbot in their newly occupied religious house. The turncoat monk did the deed and the soldiers marched in. The peaceful religious men did not put up very much opposition and soon calm was restored. The traitorous monk was indeed invested as Abbot complete with mitre and cope, then they hanged him, dressed in these vestments, over the west gate of the abbey as a reward for his treachery. It is claimed that the horrific screams of the monk being dragged to his execution have been heard, and a complete re-enactment of those final, horrible moments has been seen on 25th May, the anniversary of the event.

POTTER HEIGHAM
The Phantom Bridal Carriage

The three-arched bridge at Potter Heigham is notorious for being narrow, both to those driving pleasure craft beneath it and to the vehicles crossing over it – so slight is the passageway that traffic lights have to govern the passage of cars. A structure of clear antiquity, the bridge would have been old on 31st May 1741 when Lady Evelyn Carew finally married her heart's desire, Sir Godfrey Haslitt of Bastwick, but the path to this union had not been an easy one.

Lady Evelyn had been driven to distraction by her unrequited love for Sir Godfrey. Her Christian prayers unanswered, she turned

The old bridge at Potter Heigham.

to the black arts and consulted a witch. A deal was brokered whereby Lady Evelyn would give her soul to the Devil in exchange for marriage to Sir Godfrey – at least she could enjoy her earthly life with the man she had always wanted, or so she thought.

The Devil does not play fair and no time was stipulated on the contract. Yes, she did have the marriage of her dreams but at midnight on the same day the Devil came to collect. Seized from her marital bed by demons, she was dragged kicking and screaming to a waiting coach pulled by four black horses. Whipped up by a skeletal coachman, they took the carriage along the road at breakneck speed, foaming at their bits and with their hooves thundering. At Potter Heigham bridge the diabolical entourage crashed into the stonework and the carriage smashed into matchwood as it hit the river Thurne in an eruption of boiling water and brimstone. No trace of Lady Evelyn's body was ever found but the whole horrible event is said to be repeated in ghostly form, sounds and all, at midnight every year on 31st May, the anniversary of the tragedy.

· WEST NORFOLK AND KING'S LYNN ·

CASTLE RISING
Queen Isabella

Queen Isabella is known to history as the 'She-Wolf of France' after her fiery temper and the treatment of her husband Edward II in 1327. Following a rebellion led by her lover Roger Mortimer, Queen Isabella is alleged to have attempted to kill Edward through starvation and by leaving him in a stinking hole of a dungeon in Berkeley Castle, where the stench of putrefied carcasses from the room below filled the air he breathed. But he lingered on. After eight months Isabella was complicit in his murder. The idea was that no mark was to be left on the King's body, so a red-hot poker was inserted up his anus and he died horrifically as his bowels burnt, blistered and burst. Isabella's son soon took the throne but did not thank his mother or her lover for their deed. Mortimer was executed for treason but the young Edward III relented on his mother and had her removed to Castle Rising. Historical evidence indicates that Isabella lived her life at Rising in comfort as the Dowager Queen, with servants and ladies in waiting, but the stipulation was that she should never show her face in public again. Some accounts, however, go on to say that as time passed the Queen became increasingly deranged, taking to walking the battlements lamenting her life, wailing for

Castle Rising, the comfortable 'prison' of Queen Isabella.

her dead lover and screaming at her fate. Could it be that she suffered from what we understand today as manic depression?

Although Queen Isabella was eventually moved to Hertford Castle, where she died in 1358, it was not long after her death that

The steps in the keep of Castle Rising where visitors have been passed by a young mother and toddler in medieval clothes only to look again and find they have disappeared.

reports were made of her ghastly screams being heard from her old home at Castle Rising. A ghostly wolf with burning red eyes was also reported, its unearthly howls emanating from the battlements on the night of full moon. There have been accounts of the phantom screams and child-like weeping being heard at the castle up to very recent years, and now cold spots and unexplained sudden gusts of wind in odd places around the enclosed rooms of the castle are increasingly being experienced.

Another report tells of how an apparently solid woman and toddler in medieval dress have been seen descending the main flight of steps to the entrance door inside the castle. One visitor and her 11-year-old son saw the medieval woman and child pass them, the mother being careful to hold the child's hand as it toddled down from step to step. They simply thought the woman and young child were part of a medieval re-enactment group. Moments after the mother and toddler had carefully stepped past, and wondering if some special event was taking place, the visiting mother turned to ask but the woman and child had simply disappeared. The visitors ran down the steps to look outside across the green of the castle but the woman and toddler could not be seen and after making enquiries they were told there were no special events planned for that day.

King's Lynn
The Witch's Heart

As a historian of ghosts, witches and folklore it would be remiss of me not to point out that, contrary to popular belief, most witches executed in the British Isles were hanged rather than burned. Indeed, most women who faced the flames in this country were burnt for crimes such as petty treason

A burning at the stake.

The heart above the window in the Tuesday Market Place, King's Lynn.

and forgery. As ever, there are exceptions and one of a handful to be found across the eastern counties was Mary Smith, who was burnt for witchcraft in the Tuesday Market Place in King's Lynn on 12th January 1616.

The circumstances of this case are the subject of the rare contemporary tract entitled *A Treatise of Witchcraft* by Alexander Roberts BD, a 'Preacher of Gods Word at Kings-Linne'. Mary was the wife of Henry Smith, a glover in the town. She occupied herself making and selling cheese but, seemingly jealous of the proficiency, quality and success of others in the trade, she was alleged to have set about cursing them through a pact with the Devil. Her wrath knew no bounds when John Orkton, a sailor, struck her son following a misdemeanour. She cursed him that 'his fingers might rotte off' and, lo, within nine months his fingers were so infected that they had to be amputated.

Following similar misfortunes wished on others, Mary was tried as a witch and her black cat was declared a 'familiar'. She was found guilty. Such was the belief in her repentance while she awaited her fate in gaol that when the fatal day came the crowds sung psalms rather than jeered her on her way to the stake. It is even said that the heart carved above one of the windows in the market place marks the spot where, when the flames were at their highest, her own heart flew out from her body and smashed onto the wall. Some said that this was a sign of true repentance and purity – but others declared it to be a final curse against the magistrate who had sent her to her doom, the organ having smashed into the lintel above the window where the justice lived. The house where the heart is carved may well have been the subject of her curse too, as doors inexplicably slam shut or open of their own accord while ghostly footsteps and mutterings have also been heard about the building.

Raynham Hall and Houghton Hall
The Brown Lady

No book on the ghosts of Norfolk would be complete without reference to the 'Brown Lady' seen in both Raynham and Houghton Halls. The ghost, so named because of the brown brocade dress she always wears, is supposed to be Dorothy Walpole – sister of Sir Robert Walpole, the man regarded as the first British Prime Minister, the owner of Houghton Hall, and the wife of agriculturalist Viscount Charles 'Turnip' Townshend of Raynham Hall. Since her death on 29th March 1726 she has frequently been seen at both great houses, around their estates and even on the road between South and West Raynham.

She has appeared to many, regardless of social status or rank. No lesser man than the Prince Regent (later George IV) encountered her when he was staying in the State Bedroom at Houghton. Although it was night-time, he declared: 'I will not pass another hour in this accursed house, for I have seen that what I hope to God I may never see again.' Others recorded as having seen her include one Major Loftus in 1849 – an event that is mentioned in *Rifts in the Veil* by Lucia Stone. A number of people were staying at Raynham at the time and Loftus saw the Brown Lady on two consecutive nights. On the first night he spotted her in the corridor and he followed her a little way before she disappeared. On the second night he met her face to face. 'She was wearing a richly brocaded brown dress and a sort of coif on her head. Where her eyes should have been, nothing but dark hollows were visible.' Captain Marryat, the creator of *Mr Midshipman Easy*, also saw the Brown Lady when he was staying at Raynham. He boldly fired a

Houghton Hall.

pistol at the figure. She instantly disappeared and the bullet was found embedded in the door behind where she had stood.

In more modern times motor racing legend Sir Henry 'Tim' Birkin was disturbed and sat up in bed during the 1920s. He saw nothing, but his dog showed signs of acute terror in the small hours. The Marchioness Townshend stated in *True Ghost Stories* (1936) that when her son George and a friend were small boys they had met the Brown Lady on the staircase and had been distressed because they did not understand why they could see the stairs right through her! During the Second World War her appearance on the road caused the service police at the military base of West Raynham to chase her through the blackout, but she just disappeared into the darkness.

Raynham Hall, still the private home of the Townshend family.

Undoubtedly her best ever attested appearance of more modern times was on 19th September 1936 at 4 o'clock in the afternoon, when Captain Provand and his assistant, Indre Shira, were in the process of photographing Raynham Hall for a feature in *Country Life*. Provand had already taken one shot and was preparing for a second when Shira noticed a misty form apparently descending the stairs. Shira's account published in the December edition described the incident: 'Rather excitedly I called out "Quick! Quick! There's something! Are you ready?" "Yes," the photographer replied, and removed the cap from the lens. I pressed the trigger on the flashlight pistol. After the flash, and on closing the shutter, Captain Provand removed the focusing cloth from his head and, turned to me, said: "What's all the

The famous photograph of the ghost on the stairs at Raynham Hall.

excitement about?"' Shira explained what he saw but Provand, a former court photographer, dismissed such a thing. However, in the darkroom the misty form was revealed on the negative. Shira wanted a third witness to the developing and ran down get chemist Benjamin Jones, the manager of the premises below, as witness and all three attested to the fact that the negative had not been tampered with in any way. Today the misty image of the Brown Lady on Raynham staircase has been reproduced many times and scientifically tested by increasingly advanced methods over the years. No tampering has been detected and the image remains one of the most convincing photographs of a ghost of all time.

SNETTISHAM
The Restless Dead

One of the most fascinating cases in the annals of British ghosts was recorded and published in the *Proceedings of the Society for Psychic Research* in 1895, and it includes dates, times, places and depositions from many of those involved. The case dated back to 1878 when a certain Mrs Seagrim, a native of Snettisham, was suffering from an illness and it was considered that a trip to stay at her sister's house at 5 Rodney Place, Clifton in Kent would prove beneficial. Sadly she did not recover, but died on 22nd December 1878 after just three days' residence.

Almost fifteen years later the house at Clifton had been leased to a Mr and Mrs Ackland, and their friend Mrs Goodeve had come to stay with her two small children on 4th October 1893. At about 1.15 am on 9th October Mrs Goodeve was awoken by a cold wind blowing over her face. She first looked at the door and window; both were closed but as her eyes wound around the room she

Snettisham church.

became aware of the translucent figure of a woman leaning over her. Her ghostly visitor appeared to be wearing nightclothes with a white shawl over her head and shoulders. Her features, although kindly, looked ill and emaciated. The figure spoke in a clear voice: 'Follow me.' Mrs Goodeve followed her to the dining room where the figure turned and said, 'Tomorrow.'

It seems Mrs Goodeve was probably a psychic, or at least comfortable with visitors from the spirit world. She calmly related the tale to the Acklands who thought the spirit answered the description of the unfortunate lady who had died in the house

The grave of Henry Barnard in Snettisham churchyard.

years before and they suggested she discuss the matter with Dr Marshall who had attended Mrs Seagrim. They all agreed that the likeness tallied. The following night Mrs Goodeve attempted to stay up and sat in a chair reading, but fell asleep. At around midnight she awoke to find the same spirit of the woman she now believed to be Mrs Seagrim standing beside her. The agitated spirit was accompanied by two other figures, one a tall, well built man of about 60 who gave his name as Henry Barnard and said he was buried in Snettisham churchyard. The third spirit, another man, appeared with his head buried in his hands and seemed to be suffering great misery.

The spirit of Mr Barnard told Mrs Goodeve the dates of his marriage and death and asked her to go to Snettisham. If she found the dates correct she was to visit the church at 1.15 am and wait by the grave of Robert Cobb in the south-west corner of the south aisle where she would be given another message. Barnard's spirit also made a prediction that Mrs Goodeve would arrive at Snettisham station after dark, she would not be asked for her ticket and a dark man would help her. He would confirm that he was the person intended by telling her that his young son had been drowned. The three ghosts then faded away.

As the spirits departed Mrs Goodeve began to feel faint and only just managed to ring the bell to summon Mrs Ackland to her aid before she collapsed to the floor.

Mrs Goodeve recovered well enough to set out on her journey. Returning to London the following morning, she bought a ticket but missed the early train and had to catch a later one, which caused her to arrive after dark, as per the prediction. It was late when she arrived at Snettisham and nobody asked for her ticket; although the ticket collector was on duty neither he nor Mrs Goodeve saw one another. Arriving too late for admission to local hotels, Mrs Goodeve chanced to meet John Bishop, the church clerk, who was still dressed in the long black cassock he wore for church duties. He welcomed the visitor to his home where he and his wife offered her a room. During the course of the evening Mrs Goodeve found out their son had died in a tragic bathing accident – without doubt John Bishop was the man in black who was going to help her.

She told him of her mission and he willingly agreed to assist with her visit to the church, as long as they had permission from the curate. In daylight they went to visit the curate. When checked, the dates in the registers all tallied with what the spirit of Henry Barnard had told her. Mrs Goodeve's claims and request seemed so preposterous to the curate, however, that he refused to be involved; but he did say John Bishop had a key and could do as he saw fit.

That evening Mrs Goodeve attended evensong at the church but wondered if she really did have the nerve to complete the task given her from beyond the grave. In the small hours of the following morning Bishop, the clerk, led Mrs Goodeve to the church, let her in, locked the door behind her and left her in pitch darkness. At 1.40 am, in accordance with her request, Bishop gave three taps on the door and let her out. She never revealed what happened within those stone walls over those 25 minutes – we can only know what she did next.

First she went to Henry Barnard's grave and plucked a white rose from a bush that grew there. The following morning she took the flower to his daughter, who lived in a house located between Snettisham and Ingoldisthorpe. Here, Mrs Goodeve also passed on a message to the daughter given to her in the church. She then returned home.

Neither Mrs Goodeve nor the daughter of Henry Barnard ever publicly revealed the message passed to them. Anthony C. Wilson in his article on the subject for *Norfolk Fair* in 1975 conjectured: 'It was not clear who the third phantom was, nor exactly how Mrs Seagrim was involved, but there is a significant link between the Barnards and the Cobbs. Park House, to which Mrs Goodeve took the white rose, had previously been known as Cobb Hall and was the residence of Robert Cobb by whose grave she had waited. There was also a vague reference in the account to "forgiveness". It seems, therefore, that some great wrong had been committed, and those implicated could not rest until the matter had been put right.' Mr Wilson was in no doubt in his conclusion that the statements made by all concerned make this 'one of the best authenticated ghost stories of all time'.

GREAT MELTON
The Ghosts of Bow Hill

At the Great Melton end of Bow Hill Lane there once stood the renowned local landmark where Sir Edward Lombe's harriers used to meet – the ancient Great Melton Beech. Under the tree, it was said, the ghost of a deeply distressed weeping woman could be seen at every midnight, rocking back and forth as she nursed a phantom baby.

Further along this road towards the B1108 is Bow Hill (OS Explorer 237: GR 1206); on the left-hand side there was said to have been a deep pit or hole full of water, locally reputed to be fathomless. A long-told tale associated with this area is that of a phantom coach, which careers off the road and disappears into the pit. As with any story handed down from generation to generation by the fireside, elements tend to get embroidered. I will limit my account to two versions of what folklore tells us about the manifestation. One tale recounts how the coach was filled with bridesmaids who had had more than enough to drink to celebrate the happy union they had just attended – the trouble was that so had the coachman! He lost control of the speeding coach, causing it to swerve off the road and into a roadside pit, said by many to be bottomless, where coach, horses and passengers all sank and

Bow Hill at Great Melton.

perished. The second version tells that the coach was held up by a highwayman who killed the coachman and the pretty passengers and dumped them in that same bottomless pit. Either way, the terrible sight of a phantom carriage and four, containing four women in white, was said to be seen rising dripping from the pit every day, not only at 12 midnight but also 12 noon. It should also be remembered: 'If you see their pretty faces, all is well, but if they are headless beware, for it presages disaster.' Once risen, the coach, sprites and all, would 'flit stately and silently' round the nearby field 'divided from the Yare by a slip of plantation where local tradition says the old Norwich Road used to run'. When the run is over the coach returns to the pit and sinks silently into it again.

Although the fathomless pit appears to have magically dried up and become filled in, Bow Hill certainly has an 'atmosphere' about it. There have been no reliable sightings of the coach in recent years but the disembodied clatter of hooves and iron-shod wheels have been reported on several occasions. We visited the area on a sunny autumn day and walked through the trees that have grown on the site where the pit was supposed to have been. Although there was a breeze, one area was considerably colder than others. If you don't believe me, go and see. Your journey will not be wasted in any case, as the Barford Cock, one of the best pubs for a warm welcome, local ales and superb food, is just around the corner!

LODDON
Snuffy's Ghost

Eddie Mitchell was a great character, a tall ex-Grenadier Guardsman and in every way a true son of Norfolk. Although this may be the county with the greatest number of ghosts, sturdy Norfolk men often shrug off such talk as nonsense or save it just to frighten the 'young 'uns' round the fire during the winter months; but Eddie swore this tale was true.

When he was a lad aged about seven in 1922, his father, Edmund Paul Mitchell, had the cobbler's shop in the corner of Church Plain in Loddon. On a Saturday night Mr Mitchell senior kept his shop open until about 8 pm, hoping folks would come in for their boots and shoes and he would have a few extra shillings to give his wife for the weekend. The Mitchells lived at Chedgrave, and on a Saturday night young Eddie and his mother would walk down to the cobbler's shop to collect his father and continue down The Street to the King's Head, run in those days

The King's Head at Loddon.

by Mr and Mrs Richard Alexander, where they would meet their friends and neighbours, Mr and Mrs Scrivener. Eddie's father did not drink, being a strict teetotaller, but he liked a smoke, while Eddie's mother would have a gin, and because lads as young as Eddie were not allowed in the bar they would all sit in Mrs Alexander's kitchen.

On this particular night Mr Mitchell was on his way to the bar to get the drinks in and as ever 'Snuffy' Balls (known to all by this *nom-de-guerre* because of the copious amounts of powerful snuff he was always taking) was there too. Everyone knew Snuffy, he was a character in his own right. As choirmaster at Chedgrave church he also assisted at christenings, marriages and funerals – so everyone had contact with him, literally, from the cradle to the grave. His dress was also seen by the locals as eccentric, as he wore a long black cloak and a black hat that Eddie described as being 'rather like that of a Canadian mountie'. Regular as clockwork he, too, would be down the King's Head on a Saturday night for his pint.

This being a cold, pitch black and very blustery February night, a few ghostly tales had no doubt been shared over the pub kitchen table, so when Mr Mitchell was being served and saw Mr Balls was also waiting at the bar he casually said to him, in a typically Norfolk way of enquiring, 'They tell me your cottage is haunted, Snuffy.' To which the old man freely replied, 'Well, it is.' Mr Mitchell voiced the view of the sceptic, saying 'A lot o' people say thass a load o' squit.' Undaunted by the chide, Snuffy suggested 'Why don't you come along and see it for yourself then?' Not really knowing what to expect, Mr Mitchell took Snuffy up on his offer and returned to the kitchen. Mrs Mitchell asked where the drinks were but he replied, with a twinkle in his eye, by telling his family and friends to get their scarves and hats on – 'We're gorn up Snuffy's cottage.' The group knew full well the purpose of the visit and soon they were leaving the warm kitchen and venturing out into the cold, wet and windy night.

Snuffy did not live far away; the cottage he shared with his sister was up a cul-de-sac near the pub, which backed onto Loddon marshes. Eddie remembers that the building was very old, ancient even, and Snuffy pulled out a key about nine inches long to open the back door.

Once inside Snuffy turned up the lamp and pulled out chairs for his guests and they all sat quietly round the table near the fire. They were all a little edgy. The wind was blowing gusts of rain against the windows, causing the frames to rattle. Snuffy sensed the impatience of the group and warned them, 'There's no tellin'

– she might not come tonight.' But they did sit there a while longer. Mr Scrivener was particularly uncomfortable with the atmosphere of anticipation. Suddenly, there was a metallic click; everyone turned towards the sound and through the gloom the lamplight shone just enough for them to see a small door down the other end of the room. As their eyes strained to see in the darkness, a woman's lace bonnet came through the door – nobody wearing it, just the bonnet. It looked as if it was being worn by someone who was completely invisible. It came so close to the fire that Snuffy had to pull his chair in. Down went the bonnet as if the unseen figure was bending, and to the fearful fascination of those riveted to their seats, an invisible hand picked up the poker, stoked the fire with it and replaced it carefully back on the grate. The bonnet then rose again as if the figure was standing, watching the fire, for what seemed like an eternity but was probably in fact just a few seconds. It then drifted back down the other side of the table to the door. The latch sprung open with the same click and the bonnet went out again – carefully closing the door behind it.

With the final closure of the door a pregnant pause descended over the group. Mr Scrivener had been frightened enough and firmly suggested they should all return to the pub for a stiff drink – he bought one for Snuffy too. As Eddie concluded, 'Nobody took the mickey out o' Snuffy's ghost after that!'

NORWICH CASTLE
Hatred Beyond the Grave?

Norwich City has been dominated by its Norman castle atop its tall mound for almost a thousand years. First a fortification and a symbol of the conquerors' assumption of power and governance, in the 12th century part of

Norwich Castle atop its high mound.

the castle became a prison and by the 14th century the whole building was being used as the county gaol. Executions such as burning at the stake were carried out in the castle ditches, and on the approach to the main gate, on the bridge over the ditches, the scaffold would be erected where felons were executed by hanging. Over the years hundreds went to their doom here and one would assume that there were many spirits haunting these historic walls. There are surprisingly few recorded, however, although one manifestation does seem to recur.

Over almost 200 years and up to the year of writing, staff and visitors have reported occasional sightings of a lady dressed in black, early 19th century, clothes whose figure floats eerily through the art exhibition area inside the castle and glides smoothly around the castle mound. The possible lineage of this haunting may be traceable back to 1820 when a complaint was lodged in the prison that a number of prisoners had been terrified by a manifestation of 'something indescribable', which passed over their cell-bound recumbent bodies during the small hours of the morning.

Sadly this early account was not more specific but my research has turned up a possible candidate for the floating lady in black – a certain Martha Alden, who lived in a modest cottage with her husband Samuel in Attleborough. Apparently, arguments between this couple got progressively worse and more and more frequent over the period of about three years. On 18th July 1807 Samuel Alden was tucked up sound asleep in his bed, merrily snoring his head off. Martha was, so she claimed, 'seized with a sudden mania' during which she grabbed a bill-hook and leapt upon her recumbent husband. In a frenzied attack she hacked at his head, neck and throat with the tool, causing hideous mutilations and fatal wounds.

The attack may have been carried out in a 'sudden mania' but she carefully considered her subsequent actions. The next day, with the collusion of a girl named Mary Orvice, Mrs Alden removed Samuel's body to a dry ditch in the garden. On the 20th the two women managed to get the corpse into a corn sack and carried it to the nearby common where they slid it into a pond. Subsequently the body was discovered from its clumsy concealment, and was soon identified as Sam Alden. Martha was arrested on suspicion of murder and taken away to stand trial. She did not have to wait long. On 27th July 1807 she was tried at the Norfolk Assizes before Mr Justice Grose. In summing up, the Judge meted out a severe warning to Mary Orvice, whom he considered most fortunate in that she had not been charged with being accessory to an attempted concealment of murder. No mercy was shown to Martha Alden; found guilty of murdering her husband, she was sentenced to the full rigour of the law and condemned to death.

In those days before football matches, film shows and television a hanging was a real 'event'. Literally thousands of spectators from Norwich and its environs would attend such public executions, some travelling many miles. On the day of Martha Alden's execution, 31st July 1807, a rowdy throng from Attleborough attended en masse – they were not going to miss the final humiliations and death of their local murderess. Crowds spread across the horse and cattle market. Temporary wooden stands were built to enable grandstand views and premiums were paid by gentry wishing to rent private rooms in buildings affording the best views of the scaffold. As the onlookers drew around 'long song sellers' offered broadsheets recounting the story of the murder in words, pictures and poetry. Gin wagons sold brews by the cup while the hawkers of hot pies, pastries and fancies did a good trade (as did the pickpockets who managed quite a haul of purses and pocket watches).

Alden was drawn from the prison to her place of execution in Norwich Castle ditches on a hurdle (a type of agricultural fence panel rustically woven in wood). This was a real mark of shame which was reserved for the worst criminals such as murderers and traitors. Her treatment can be said to reflect the punishment sometimes described as 'petty treason', from the notion that every household was a microcosm of the kingdom with master and mistress being king and queen, children young princes and princesses, and down through the strata to servants who were their obedient and loyal people. Any breach of this system could incur severe punishments; servant girls who let thieving boyfriends in to

*A contemporary print of the execution of Martha Alden
in front of Norwich Castle on 31st July 1807.*

steal the family plate could face the penalty of burning at the stake. In the eyes of the law Martha Alden had also committed her own petty treason – the 'Queen' had killed her 'King'!

On Martha's arrival at the scaffold an expectant hush fell over the crowd. As she approached the gallows cries of 'Hats off' were heard – this was not a mark of respect, as the call requested headgear to be removed to allow better views for those further back. The murderess was 'swung' before a huge assembly of people, her life ending on the hangman's rope, but her punishment did not end with death. After her body was cut down from the gallows it was handed over to the surgeons for dissection. So angry were the residents of Attleborough at Martha's crime that a mob showed their detestation by destroying the cottage she had shared with her husband.

A few days after the execution, the first reports appeared claiming that a ghostly figure identified as Martha Alden had been spotted walking on Castle Hill. In the month of December 1807 a party of men set out from Attleborough to hide upon the mount and wait for the spectre to appear. They were prepared to try to 'lay' the spirit by bell, book and scripture. The trouble was that the ghost was a long time appearing and in the meantime they all took a little too much 'Dutch courage' to calm their nerves and became roaring drunk. That was to be the only spirit around that night and the men were seized by the jailer and detained in prison for two days pending an enquiry into their conduct. They certainly did not 'lay' Martha's spirit, so could it be that it is her ghost that still wanders, repentant and lost, around the mound of Norwich Castle today?

SHOTESHAM
The Village Vampire

This story has been pieced together from a chance discovery of a series of events recorded as and when they happened in a handwritten household book of recipes, country cures and significant events from a small group of villages to the south of Norwich. The book itself dates back over 225 years and, judging by the different styles of handwriting and occasional dates, it was maintained over about three or four generations. These volumes are in a private collection but I have had privileged access to see the originals first-hand. In what follows, the place names are exactly as they were spelt in the original account and contemporary documents.

In the early 19th century the area known as Low Shottesham comprised the parishes of Shottesham St Mary, St Martin and St Botolph. Out of the four hundred or so people who lived in the parish most folk worked on the big estate of Shottesham Park in the employ of Robert Fellowes Esq, or on the land of the neighbouring farmers.

Life was simple and the medical assistance available to ordinary country people was limited to say the least. Few could afford the attendance of a physician and many turned to the local 'cunning man or woman' to provide the cures when home-made poultices and herb-based medicines failed. There were still many who believed in witches and witchcraft and they would consult the local 'Mother' on more esoteric matters such as finding love, falling pregnant or desiring a good crop for the year. When apparently contagious illness struck such rural village areas, the fears and suspicions of locals were often heightened. People would be terrified of the sickness passing to them and would turn to witches' charms to ward off the infection from their door. Thus, occurrences that were slightly out of the ordinary could easily be blown up out of all proportion into 'the work of the Devil's hand'. Perhaps this is what happened here.

One unfortunate household consisted of a hard-working father, a labourer on one of the local farms, and a mother who had at least four children of a young age at home. Several of the children fell ill with a mystery sickness. No potion or treatment offered by the local sources seemed to provide any relief for the sickness, which bore a great similarity to the dreaded smallpox. The children initially suffered 'melancholy', then progressively intense stomach pains and vomiting. The locals really started to fear the worst when 'a bright red rash' appeared over the children's bodies and they began to hallucinate, seeing creatures 'flying about the walls'. The curious thing was that the children did not seem to exhibit the fever that normally accompanies smallpox, and neither did the mother when she contracted the symptoms – but within ten days mother and children were all dead. This may be a useful point in the story to mention, just in passing, that the symptoms recorded as being suffered by this family bear similarities to those caused by a naturally occurring poison such as that contained in *Atropa belladonna* – the deadly nightshade plant.

By some apparent cruel twist of fate the father, despite having faithfully tended to his stricken family, showed no symptoms of the sickness whatsoever, and neither did anyone else in the village. Despite the poor man being distraught at his loss there was little comfort from the locals who ostracised him for fear he might pass the mysterious sickness on to them. He was also a changed man; some folks even went so far as to say that his family had been cursed or that he had entered into a pact with the Devil to save his own soul, since after all he had been seen consulting the local witches. The gossips apparently did not consider the fact that he was probably the only member of the family well enough to do so and a desperate father would try anything to save his family.

It was around this time that animals on a couple of local farms were found dead or dying at sun-up, with severe cuts delivered about their bodies; one had horribly aborted her foetus calf. As ever, when fear still lingers, the fingers will begin to point at a scapegoat – and fingers began to point at the man who had recently lost his family. Although there was no specific mention of the word 'vampire' in the text from which this account is drawn it was clearly pointed out that blood, dried and worn about the person in a small corked jar, had been a known ward against plague and other epidemic diseases. Was it just malicious gossip that claimed the poor man was drinking the fresh blood of the cattle in an attempt to purge himself of the killer sickness he thought he carried?

The man who had survived when all his family perished was clearly (to some of the locals) 'overlooked by witches'; to modern eyes the behaviour he displayed was akin to mental illness. He took to wandering about at night, and those who saw him in daylight reported that he seemed panicky and twitchy, and appeared on occasion 'to spin on his heels as if he heard somebody, unseen and unheard by others, call to him'. It all became too much and this troubled man walked off to a local wood and took his own life by cutting his throat.

Until the 1850s people who committed suicide were not always buried in consecrated ground but rather a separate, distant area in the shadowy north of the churchyard where the body would be laid face down, facing west – that was if they were lucky. Many believed that the restless spirits of those who took their own lives would 'walk' to harass those they left behind, and they would be buried away from the town or village at a four-way crossroads so the ghost would not know which path to take to return.

This was what was decided upon in the case of the poor bereaved man. The ground was hard at the Shottesham crossroads and the church sexton soon sweated as he began to spade out the earth for the pit. Brought to the crossroads and without any Christian ceremony, the body was dropped into the deep hole at dusk. The local blacksmith assisted the sexton to fix a chain, and nails were driven through the joints. A small crowd gathered around to witness the deed. In all cases of such horrible rites the final act was to drive an oaken stake through the heart of the poor soul being so buried, to ensure that the body and ghost stayed down by being 'pinned' (a practice prohibited by Act of Parliament in 1823). On this occasion it was noted that the deed was made more horrible by the 'effusion of black blood from the body'.

But, curiously, sporadic attacks on the animals still occurred on odd occasions over the next few months, usually on the night of the full moon when, perhaps coincidentally, an indistinct figure was spotted nearby at very odd times during the hours of darkness. Nobody could get close enough to obtain a good description of the figure, apart from the impression that it appeared to be 'more of a shadow than a man'. Did the ghost of the poor man driven mad by the loss of his family and persecution by locals rise and walk again to haunt those who had treated him so badly? It is interesting to speculate that a series of tragic events and unconnected malicious attacks by others at a time when local society was vulnerable and frightened may have resulted in an innocent man taking his own life.

· BRECKLAND AND THETFORD ·

BRANDON
'A Navie ... in the Ayre'

One of the strangest accounts of paranormal phenomena is recorded in a rare tract entitled *Signes from Heaven, or severall Apparitions seene and hearde in (the) Ayre in the Counties of Cambridge and Norfolk, on 21st day of May last past in the afternoon 1646.* Perhaps this curious pamphlet was an allegory or maybe this spectacular occurrence really did take place in the skies over Norfolk, I leave readers to decide for themselves. Before it is dismissed out of hand, however, do consider other, similar, large-scale manifestations such as the Battle of Edgehill, which was fought in 1642 and replayed in the skies above the battlefield with such frequency that King Charles sent three officers and three 'gentlemen of credit' to witness it. The officers had been involved in the fighting on the actual day of the battle and recognised many of the spectral clashes and even some of the combatants.

The relevant section of the four-page pamphlet is recorded here verbatim:

Also at Brandon, in the County of Norfolke, the inhabitants were forced to come out of their houses to behold so strange a

A phantom battle in the sky from a 17th century broadsheet.

spectacle of a spire steeple ascending up from the earth, and a pike or lance descending downwards from Heaven. The Lorde in Mercy blesse and preserve His Church, and settle peace and truth among all degrees, and more especially among our churchmen ... In Brandon in the county aforesaid, was seen at the same time a navie or fleet of ships in the ayre, swiftly passing under sayle, with flags and streamers hanged out, as if they were ready to give an encounter ... In Marshland, in the county of

Norfolk aforesaid, within three miles of King's Linne, a Captain
and a Lieutenant, with divers other persons of credit, did heare,
in the time of thunder, a sound as of a whole regiment of drums
beating a call, with perfect notes and stops, much admired at of
all that heard it.

BRECKLES
The End of George Mace, the Poacher

B reckles Hall is situated on the edge of Breckland in South
Norfolk. The present building is mostly of 16th century
construction and was the scene of many anxious times
when the Wodehouse family remained sympathetic to the old
Roman Catholic religion after it was abolished in England by
Henry VIII. Francis Wodehouse's third wife, Eleanor, was a
particularly loyal papist; she was fined on a number of occasions
for not attending church and the hall was frequently searched in
the belief that they harboured priests. The fines levied against the
Wodehouse family eventually proved too much and they had to
sell Breckles Hall.

Perhaps that is when the hall acquired a curse for, as the
antiquarian Dr Augustus Jessop (see the Mannington Hall story,
page 39) pointed out, it became 'a house which for 300 years, no
owner seems to have been able to hand down to a grandson of his
own'. It was also a house in which two of its owners are said to have
died in mysterious circumstances, driven by unseen forces and bad
fortune to take their own lives. Over the years the hall had fallen
into disrepair and acquired stories of mysterious lights being seen
there when there was no known occupant. Some even said that on
certain nights in the month of December, a spectral coach was to
be seen galloping up the drive.

The driveway to Breckles Hall.

One fatal night in a December in the early 19th century a band of poachers set out to 'walk by night' and bag some game from the grounds. As they left the pub where they met, one old local spluttered into his pint and told them to look out for the coach, but these were country men – they most certainly did not believe in ghosts and were not going to be deterred from their quest to bag a brace or two of 'longtails' (pheasants) for the Christmas table.

The hardest and most senior of the band of poachers, George Mace, was elected their look-out man and they arranged to meet at the dilapidated hall to divide their spoils after a couple of hours of poaching. Mace was already at the porch of the hall as they walked to meet him. The church clock struck twelve but they stopped in their tracks the instant the final chime began to fade as an eerily glowing spectral coach swept silently up the drive. Rooted to the ground by fear, the men stared in horror as the coach halted in front of the porch and the ghostly apparition of a lady, beautifully dressed in a ball gown, with powdered face and hair piled high, stepped from it. The windows of the great hall seemed to glow with a greenish tinged candlelight. They could clearly see that Mace had flattened himself to the wall but terror caused him to freeze to the spot. The spectral lady was seen to stare straight into Mace's eyes – he slumped to the ground with a blood-curdling shriek that cut through the night air.

The scream seemed to release his friends from their transfixed state and they ran to the nearest house to get help but could find no-one willing to go near the hall until daylight. Next morning the poachers returned to the spot along with the vicar and a group of villagers. In front of the hall they found the body of poor George Mace. He lay stiff and cold, his face twisted into a mask of terror.

HOCKWOLD FENS
The Lost Warriors

In many cases ghosts seem to have a purpose; frequently their manifestation relates to a dramatic or tragic event in the past, almost a kind of *memento mori*, so it is made all the more tragic when the mists of time have obscured or lost the story behind the haunting. Long before the discovery of the Hockwold Hoard of Roman silver the Fens were said to have been haunted by the ghostly figures of ancient warriors whose calls and even an apparent 'sound of battle' have drifted across the misty wetlands. Suggestions have been put forward for some fracas being fought here – perhaps the Iceni were defending their land and the treasure they had stolen from the Roman invaders, or maybe those who knew where the treasure was were all slain and their spirits returned to haunt their booty. Another account tells of how the spirits are some of Kett's rebels of 1549 who were hounded to ground here after the defeat of the peasant protest force at Dussinsdale in Norwich.

SWAFFHAM
One for the Ladies?

There has been a hostelry on the site of the George Hotel at Swaffham since the 18th century. Enlarged and made a coaching inn with the coming of the turnpike, the oldest wing of the hotel has experienced ghostly activity from a spirit who has become affectionately known to staff as the 'Green Lady'. She appears to be dressed in early 19th century dress – green in colour – and carries something that resembles a pan in her hand. Curiously she seems to be seen most frequently by women and young children. She has been glimpsed in the lounge area and kitchen and gliding along the corridors, but her most dramatic appearances have been made in the bedrooms of the hotel in the small hours of the morning, as in the case of an American family who knew nothing of the ghost. The parents were mystified when their children, who had been sleeping in an adjoining room, asked over breakfast about the lady who had visited them in the night.

They had awoken to see her standing at the end of the bed. She was quite benign and unthreatening and they had unconcernedly gone back to sleep.

The Green Lady is not always seen but her presence is often felt. When I spoke to Helen Brumpton, the Operations Manager of the hotel, in November 2006, she explained that a group of psychic investigators and mediums had just been to stay. Helen had been sceptical of ghosts when she came to work here eleven years previously but she has experienced a number of sensations that have made her think again. One incident in particular stays with her – feeling several taps on her back when nobody else was in the area where she was standing. A similar tapping was experienced by a guest on another occasion – she thought it was her husband and told him off for irritating her, but his hands were not near her back. The tapping has been reported a number of times since and Helen wondered if the Green Lady could be responsible. However, the mediums were convinced that this was the spirit of a man who knew the hotel but did not work there, and that he was waiting for another who was still there (he did not specify whether alive or as a trapped spirit) to pass over into his world.

Perhaps the sensation of a weight about their shoulders and a sudden push or stumble experienced by the mediums as they went up the hotel's old staircase also bears some relation to the haunting. Sadly there is very little history to explain the stories behind these phenomena. The spirits all seem quite happy at the George so, hopefully, as time goes on we may yet find out more about the Green Lady and if she fell – or was she pushed?

By a curious coincidence, the old Swaffham Town Hall buildings, now Swaffham Museum, are haunted by a spirit also said to be that of a woman. She has not been seen but has made her presence known on a number of occasions. Those who have experienced her find it difficult to describe the sensation, but say that you certainly know it when you start to go cold and feel *someone* is there in the room with you or passes quickly behind you, to the extent that people have turned around quickly, only to find that no-one was there. One lady who it is thought might be at the root of this spirit activity is a certain Mrs Aldiss who occupied the building with her husband when it was a private dwelling, known as Oulton House, in the first half of the 20th century. She was considered decidedly odd by many locals as she insisted on sleeping in a separate room from her husband and wandered about the house most days, for most of the time dressed only in her long nightdress.

THETFORD
The Phantom Monks

Dating from 1103–4, Thetford Priory was once one of the largest and richest religious houses in medieval East Anglia. It was founded by the rich and powerful Roger Bigod and was amply endowed by his family for generations afterwards. Supposedly a place of contemplation, peace and harmony, the priory has also had its share of miscreants and bloodshed.

Shortly after the arrival of the first monks at the priory, Prior Stephen was sent from Lewes and strove to lay firm foundations for the future of the religious community. He observed God's word thoroughly and worked for the good of his house but the Prior who followed him, another Stephen, was equally thorough in working evil. A native of Savoy, this Stephen claimed to be a relation of the Queen or have a connexion to her and assumed airs of pride from this. He regularly forgot his Matins devotion, could not be bothered to present himself at Mass and rarely appeared at canonical hours. He even made his excuses to avoid attendance at

The ruins of Thetford Priory viewed from the site of the Great West Door
of the priory church where Prior Stephen was stabbed to death.

the general chapter of their religious order at Cluny in 1240 and, if other accounts are to be believed, 'he turned the priory of Thetford into a house of debauchery' by carousing night and day with his brothers, particularly Bernard, a knight, and another, named Guiscard, whom Matthew Paris, the 13th century chronicler, described as 'clericus monstruosus'.

One of the gaunt heads on the doorway to the Prior's house in Thetford Priory.

In 1248 Prior Stephen finally met his nemesis after embarking on a vendetta against one of his newer brethren, a hot-blooded monk of Welsh birth, Stephen de Charun. This monk could no longer stand seeing the office of prior brought into disrepute and began to make waves about Stephen. The Prior decided the best course of action to deal with the increasingly sticky situation was to send Charun back to Cluny whence he had only lately come. The monk, quite reasonably, refused the pressures put on him to leave. Prior Stephen swore in a truly unbefitting manner that he was determined he would send Charun on pilgrimage and nothing was going to turn him from his decision. Just outside the Great West Door of the priory church, Charun caught up with Stephen; the monk could take it no more and 'in a passion' drew a knife and plunged it into the Prior's stomach. The attack grew frenzied and Charun managed to stab Stephen's lifeless body another three times before he could be restrained. He was arrested and handed over to the Bishop of Norwich, from whom the King claimed him and ordered that the monk be chained and have his eyes put out. The blinded Charun was then cast into the prison at Norwich Castle, where he was left to rot and eventually died.

Another shocking occurrence took place in 1313 when a rioting mob made forcible entry to the priory where they assaulted Prior Martin, his monks and servants, some of whom were horribly maimed. Several monks and servants fled to the priory church so that they might be in sanctuary, but the mob did not respect this, slew several of them by the high altar, and carried away the goods of the priory.

At the Dissolution of the Monasteries, Henry VIII was petitioned to convert the priory into a college of secular canons, but he refused and over the centuries it fell into ruin.

Could some of these incidents have caused the spectral manifestations reported at the priory ever since? The ghostly Latin chants of the monks have been overheard here many times.

Small groups of very solid monks have been seen as if processing around the presbytery at dusk and even in broad daylight. A ghostly monk, hooded, with head bent and arms tucked into his habit, has also been reported moving silently along the site of the kitchen on several occasions up to recent years. Seemingly unaware of anyone else, this monk is also uncannily solid. One mother out with her daughter at the ruins wondered if some sort of historical display or guided walk was going to be staged there and went to ask the lifelike figure but as she approached he simply disappeared – 'one second he was there, the next, in the blink of an eye, he was gone'.

The respected paranormal researcher C.J. Romer began a lifetime career and interest in ghosts at Thetford Priory in August 1987 when he and four friends saw a figure descending a staircase in the Prior's Lodge section of the ruins, dressed as a monk might be. They all assumed it was a joker playing around and ran over to the scene, only to fall through the staircase, which had no real existence. Was this a time-slip, a momentary glimpse of the past, or was it spectral replay? Either way the noble ruins of the priory stand today and are well worth seeing. You can position yourself at the remains of the Great West Door where the dissolute Prior Stephen was murdered, even mount the steps of the high altar where the sanctuary deserved by the monks was not respected and where they were slaughtered. With these stories in mind, it is hard not to feel a shiver on even the warmest days when visiting Thetford Priory.

BURGH CASTLE
The Falling Figure

Burgh Castle was built about AD 280 during the Roman occupation of Britain and was known as Gariannonum. This castle, which stood to the south, together with

The ancient walls and towers of Burgh Castle.

129

another at Caister to the north provided fortified defences either side of the wide sea inlet where Great Yarmouth stands today. Here were based rapid reaction cavalry units to intercept any who might attempt to pirate, raid or invade. The fortification at Burgh Castle enclosed a massive seven acres with four heavy defensive walls and bastions for *ballistae* (catapults). Only three walls remain today, the fourth having fallen down the slope towards the river Waveney many years ago. Like a few other ghosts in this book we can only conjecture why the apparition that is reported here appears. It is of undoubted antiquity and is said to take the form of a ghostly body wrapped in a large white flag, and appears to be flung from the ruins onto the site of the ancient foreshore every year on 3rd July.

BURGH ST PETER
Debt in Blood

Hanging on to the border of Norfolk and Suffolk, almost by the skin of its teeth, is the village of Burgh St Peter. Along the leafy green lanes a good mile from the modern village, not far from the staithe by the banks of the Waveney and above the surrounding marsh, stands the church of St Mary with its unusual tower. This was built up in the 18th century, looking quite literally like a child's building cubes and paid for by the then rector, Samuel Boycott, after the old 16th century tower had been destroyed by lightning – an act of God, or was it, perhaps, the work of a vengeful, darker mischief maker?

A curious tale has been handed down for generations in this area; it was said to date back to the late 11th century when Burgh was a simple Norman settlement. A man named Adam Morland lived on the marshes and worked a small farm. He laboured hard to support his family. His wife Martha had borne him eight children but only three were still living and Adam wanted them to have the best life he could give them. After tithes and dues were paid to the manor, however, he had little left to improve their lot. He sought counsel with local monks in their chapel; prayers were offered on his behalf but he felt he was no better off. Perhaps, in his mind, he quietly dismissed the holy men and left himself spiritually vulnerable as he wandered back towards his home.

In despair Adam sat down upon the trunk of a fallen willow and, filled with self-pity and desperation, he put his head in his hands. It was not long before he was aware of another presence. He looked up to see an old man dressed in a long woollen cloak with a cowl pulled up over his head. His face was weather-beaten, heavily lined and a long white moustache and beard cascaded from his lower face to his chest. Adam had nothing to lose and with the abandon sometimes accorded to a stranger willing to listen he explained his woes to the old man.

After listening intently, the old man smiled kindly and with a twinkle of benevolence in his eye produced a drawstring bag, which he soon revealed was full of gold coins. All Adam had to do was put his name to a deed of receipt and promise to repay his debt on a mutually agreed date, stated by some to be, by our modern calendar, 2nd May. Adam could not sign his name; some accounts of this tale state he simply had to press his thumbprint onto wax to seal the document, others say that he pricked his finger, wiped the blood over his thumb and pressed that onto the deed instead. Either way the deal was made. The money was in Adam's hand but as soon as his fingers touched the gold, to his horror he saw the old man rot and twist to become nothing more than an animated skeleton, the kindly eyes now reduced to black sockets lit by balls of fire. As this hideous apparition disappeared in a puff of sulphurous smoke the full import of what he had done stuck him – Adam had just sold his soul to the Devil!

Burgh St Peter church: beware a cowled skeletal figure in the churchyard.

The simple farmer was terrified and sought help from family, friends and clergy. He did use the money to improve his farm but he also paid for the materials for the very first church built on the site of the present St Mary's and helped to build it. The years rolled by and eventually the day for collection of the debt loomed large. A mysterious old man wrapped in a hooded cloak was seen loitering around Adam's door and the churchyard, which had been built on the site where the loan had been agreed. Perhaps it was stress or maybe Adam Morland was just worn out from all those years working on his farm and building the church, or perhaps it was divine intervention, but a few days before the debt was due to be paid the new church was consecrated by the Lord Abbot of St Benet's-at-Holm and poor Adam was claimed to have 'tooke sicke of a fever and dyede'.

As the hour approached for the debt to be paid on 2nd May, Adam's funeral cortège arrived at the church. All the strange old man with the sealed parchment in his hand could do was stand and watch it pass into the church where the burial was carried out within those sacred walls and consecrated ground. There was no way Old Nick could claim Adam's soul now. As ever, he was a bad loser and he vented his rage by causing Adam's house to burst into flames and burn with such ferocity that only a few charred fragments were left when the fire was finally extinguished. Even after the burial of Adam the old man still lingered around the graveyard. The sexton went to see if he could help him but he soon realised that the old man was not of this world and ran screaming to the vicar. Satan was sent away by means of holy water and extending a cross towards him but he seems to keep coming back on the anniversary of the due debt. It is said that he may still be seen on every May 2nd in his cowled skeletal form, loitering around the graveyard, until the Resurrection Day when he hopes to claim the long overdue soul of Adam Morland.

Belief in this phenomenon has seen clergy and parishioners pray, fast and even scatter ashes to ward away Satan but he continues to appear. In 1683 an elderly Mary Dowsell was unfortunate enough to see the apparition, which proved to be so startling an occurrence that she was stuck down with a sickness and died insane.

The last recorded appearance of the Burgh St Peter spectre was in 1929, according to Charles Sampson in his *Ghosts of the Broads*. The case he relates was that of a boating party aboard the pleasure wherry *Venturous*, consisting of businessman John Carruthers, bridge engineer Sir Alexander Taunton, the writer Spencer Meredith, George Wetherby KC, the aviator Lady Diana Oakland, the surgeon Neville Critt, Douglas Peterson JP, who was the Sheriff of Sussex, and Lord Edgar Staines FRS. They had come to visit the village on the evening of 2nd May and decided to look at the church. Carruthers picks up the story:

> On entering the gate we saw an old man hurrying in front of us, but on reaching the church porch he disappeared. We were struck by his curious walk, and after visiting the interior of the building, who should we see on emerging into the light once more but the same old man. Lord Staines called out to him 'Hi!' and he stopped, and in that moment of his turning around, we all saw he was a skeleton with a roll of dirty looking paper in his hand. He glared at us, and decamped away across the graves, and on giving pursuit, we could find no trace of him anywhere … This sepulchral person left behind a foul, loathsome stench, and we were glad to get back to the *Venturous*, where each of us wrote a précis of what we had seen in our diaries. The eight descriptions tally exactly.

Many have said that they often feel a 'cold chilly sweat' in the area of the church even in high summer. Perhaps it could be put down to imagination or it's just the wind blowing across the cool water but for me, knowing this story, this is one ghost I will not be hanging around to see!

GREAT YARMOUTH
The Bodysnatchers

The White Horse Inn, across the Plain from St Nicholas' church in Great Yarmouth, served generations of Yarmouth folk and passing trade along Northgate Street for over 300 years. It is hardly surprising that history has left its impression on worn steps, flagstones and wooden fixtures, rounded by the touch, brush and kick of customers and staff. Some parapsychologists suggest that repetition of life processes of this sort, or sudden incidents such as extreme violence, loss or sadness can also leave their mark – the 'stone tape theory' whereby such emotion can imbed itself in the walls around it and, if the conditions are right, be replayed at later dates, perhaps days, weeks, months, years or even centuries later. In September 2003 Debbie Bee, the landlady of the White Horse, and her estate agents claimed that her attempts to sell the old pub had been jinxed. They said that people wishing to buy the property had been put off because of the spirits who were alleged to inhabit it.

The collapse of a disused weighbridge outside the pub about twelve months earlier was blamed for the sudden outbreak of spirit activity. While repairing the road the workmen had filled in an old tunnel that ran from the pub and under Northgate Street towards the churchyard. From that time on strange things had begun to happen. Balls on the pool table inexplicably began to move and glasses fell from shelves without anyone being near them. Locks in the ladies' toilet malfunctioned to the extent that they had to be removed. Then quilts were found pulled off beds, when no-one had been in the room, eerie footsteps were heard crossing floors and doors slammed or opened of their own accord. A small fortune had been spent on fixing and buying new appliances after

The old White Horse inn, now private residences, Great Yarmouth.

mysterious failures of electrical equipment. Figures flitting across the building were caught in the corner of the eyes of staff and customers. Matters came to a head when a ghostly figure was spotted in the cellar; from that time on staff would only go down there in pairs.

Three mediums identified about seven different entities, including a badly burned child, a little boy, who was particularly associated with the mischief around the pub, and a weeping lady the mediums named as Mary.

Perhaps these were simply the spirits of those associated with the pub but I suggest there may be an even darker reason for the hauntings, especially when you consider that they occurred after the disturbance of the tunnel between the pub and the church. In December 1827 bodysnatching activities were detected in Great Yarmouth. George Beck, a local baker, was concerned to find his recently buried wife's grave apparently disturbed. Further investigation confirmed his worst fears; 'resurrection men' had stolen the body. Recently bereaved families had their concerns turned into nightmares when, upon investigation, about twenty graves were found to have been tampered with and at least ten of them had been robbed of their occupant. The bodysnatching gang may have received warning of the discovery of their nocturnal activities and slipped away into the darkness but their leader, Thomas Vaughan, had 'behaved ill to a young woman to whom he passed himself off as a bachelor'. And when the law officials became involved his nefarious dealings by dead of night were exposed. The rest of the gang were soon identified and the base where they packaged the bodies and hid their booty was revealed as a rented house just across the way from the graveyard off White Horse Plain in Row 6, then known as Browne's or Rackham's Row. Carting bodies across Northgate Street would have been a risky business, even if they had done so in a covered handcart. Perhaps, just perhaps they knew of the old tunnel and slipped the landlord

St Nicholas church, Great Yarmouth, viewed from Northgate Street.

a percentage for the use of his cellar or even used it as storage for a few of their cadavers!

The landlord could easily have washed his hands of any involvement, as long as no 'evidence' was found on the premises. The bodysnatchers were certainly bailed out by their employers. Among the gang members were father and son team William and Robert Barber. The son, Robert, turned King's Evidence in a plea for leniency and told how he and his father robbed the graves, packed bodies in boxes and sent them by wagon to London. He named Surgeon Astley Cooper as the final recipient of the corpses. The most adept member of the gang was a tall, strong Irishman named Murphy who handled the bodies. He had been paid twelve guineas each for at least four of the bodies from Yarmouth. A legal representative was sent to act on behalf of Vaughan for the grand sum (in those days) of £14. Vaughan was even granted by his surgeon employers 10 shillings a week for the 26 weeks he was in confinement. Murphy was also well treated and the not inconsiderable amount of £160 was paid by the surgeons for his defence at trial.

From the time of these horrible goings-on, Row 6 acquired the nickname of 'Snatchbody Row' and the church had high-railed fences erected around the churchyard to deter the repetition of the crime. Returning to recent years, the White Horse Inn was eventually sold and has been converted into private residences. (I am sure you could look at the fine exterior of the old building, but please do respect the privacy of the new inhabitants.)

Perhaps the bodysnatching connection goes some way towards an explanation of the manifestations at the White Horse. Even if, in my theory, I have maligned the old landlord it does not take a leap of the imagination to visualise the resurrection men, having been handsomely paid for their services, rolling up to this, their local pub, to drink away some of their ill-gotten gains – and maybe some of their victims followed to haunt them. The tragedy is that all the bodysnatchers are themselves dead and buried while the trapped or lost spirits to whom they denied a consecrated grave continue to haunt the area as ghosts.

The A12 Ghost

In their book *The World's Greatest Ghosts* Nigel Blundell and Roger Boar recount the instances of a hunchbacked phantom who has been spotted on the A12 between Great Yarmouth and Lowestoft in Suffolk and could have been responsible for a number of fatal and serious accidents when drivers, thinking the figure is real, swerve to avoid it. Blundell and Boar suggest that one of the first attributable victims of the spirit was a lorry driver who knew the route well and for no apparent reason had his vehicle career off the road and smash into trees in 1960. The accident proved fatal and an open verdict was recorded by the coroner as to the cause of the accident.

In 1980 a car driver who was also familiar with the road drove into trees, again for no obvious reason. Within a year of that tragedy a cyclist swerved into the path of a car – once again there seemed to be no explanation for this. Survivors of accidents in this area have claimed that they swerved to avoid a 'shadowy figure'. Andrew Cutajar (aged 19) of Lowestoft described what he saw. 'The spectre of an old man was standing in the slow lane, just looking at me. I slammed on the brakes and skidded, expecting a thud. The car went through him and hit the kerb.' When Andrew got out of his car to investigate there was no sign of anyone or anything that could have been mistaken for the old man lying on the road. Frank Colby, a former policeman, came forward to tell of his near miss on the A12 with a figure that appeared to be an old hunchbacked man with straggly hair who 'just walked across the carriageway and disappeared'. Psychic researcher Ivan Bunn from nearby Oulton Broad has offered the suggestion that the figure could be the ghost of William Balls whose body had been discovered dead of exposure during the winter of 1899 in the area of the sightings.

Vinegar Tom, the Cobholm Bogeyman

When I was at college at Great Yarmouth in the late 1980s I balanced my academic studies with a photography course. Rather than taking pictures of what I considered rather dull still-life compositions and building forms, I much preferred 'real life' or as my tutor called it 'social documentary' photographs. I walked miles, capturing images of people at work, changing townscapes, port and seaside or simply recording the folk I saw around me. I regularly visited Cobholm; in this area there were many characters, people who had worked hard all their lives for a meagre living, a story repeated again and again in the hands and faces of the older residents. Rather than just popping up and taking a photo I would usually ask the person first, introduce myself and tell them why I wanted to photograph them.

One morning I saw a very old man walking slowly along Mill Road. He had a large frame; clearly in his youth he had been a strong man, but in old age a frame was all he was and he could only walk a short distance before he had to stop for a bit and take a breather. Not wanting to startle him, I sauntered carefully beside him and bade him good mornun' in my finest Norfolk brogue. His face lit up with a big smile, although he showed no teeth – he didn't have any. He didn't know me from Adam but he greeted me like an old friend, as best he could through the wheezes. His visage was truly a picture, a landscape of life. He had shaved fairly recently, but the light stubble around his jaw line and upper lip was met with far longer unshaved hair from his cheeks, nostrils, in fact just about everywhere he should not have had hair, even his ears. He didn't mind his photo being taken and we walked a little way to a low wall where we sat down 'for a yarn'.

I have always been interested in ghosts and had heard a few tales associated with Great Yarmouth but the old man was keen to tell me about 'Vinegar Tom, the Cobholm Bogeyman'. My companion's name, it emerged, was George and he had lived in Cobholm all his life. When he was a young lad in the 1920s most people living in the area were hard-working folk who toiled in factories, on the docks and in the timber yards of Southtown and lived in the terraced streets of Cobholm. As a child George played in the streets with his mates, usually in the alleyways that ran between the backs of the terraced houses, where mothers could 'keep an eye out' as they worked in the kitchen or hung the laundry on the line in the back yard and pushed it up high to catch the breeze with a linen prop. Most children, in those days at least, were at some time or another threatened with the bogeyman if they misbehaved or did not do what they were told, especially with regard to wandering off beyond their agreed playing area. But the difference in Cobholm was that the bogeyman was real. He was known to all as 'Vinegar Tom' – and you would smell him before you saw him – because of the odour of vinegary stale sweat. His clothes, and indeed Tom himself, were never thought to have had a wash. In the summer George remembers Tom's smell changing to be more like 'mouldy Bovril – he stunk to high heaven'. That was indeed saying something in a time before spray-on deodorants and when many people had only one bath a week in a tub in front of the fire, filled with water from the copper, and then shared the water with the rest of the family!

Vinegar Tom was described as 'a bit funny', a generic term used around these parts for just about anyone suffering mental illness or being retarded in the less understanding days of the 1920s. His mother had raised him; his father was a heavy drinker and had died (or did a flit) when Tom was a little boy. Tom had never been in any employment but he would always insist he helped his Mum. When she died Tom was just 'lost' and seemed to spend his days

One of the back alleys of Cobholm. Perhaps the spirit of Vinegar Tom
still shuffles here, or maybe just his smell lingers on.

loitering around where the kids were playing. He never spoke to them. He just stood there, dressed the way he always did, rain or shine, with a battered and grease-stained wide brimmed trilby, his neck muffled up with a mangy old scarf and an equally greasy and stained coat buckled around his middle with a belt from an old mac. He seemed tubby but it could well have been the layers of old clothes he wore. What you could see of Tom's face was ruddy, framed by straggles of greasy hair, and his beady eyes were seldom clearly visible as they were often shaded by the brim of his hat. Tom's boots were also something to behold as the soles, the old leather ones just about having worn through, consisted of layers of cardboard tied around with string. He would shuffle along, almost without a sound; you would be playing and then you would catch the whiff and seemingly out of nowhere Vinegar Tom would be there, standing by the corner, just watching and watching.

Most mums would soon send Tom on his way. Malicious and non-specific stories of him from the dim and distant past were common gossip around Cobholm. His hanging round watching kids just 'wasn't right' and he would often be despatched with a flea in his ear, and a throw-away curse of 'dirty old bugger'. But Tom never gave any abuse back, he would just shuffle off – 'Vinegar Tom, the Bogeyman' was a feature of everyday life.

Funnily enough, George admitted, for such a small community, most kids did not know where Tom lived, but then I guess most of them didn't care. However, his immediate neighbours grew concerned when they had not seen him for a while, although it took a long while for their unease to be brought to the attention of the authorities; after all, he might not have been noticed going in and out of his house but the kids in the alleys and their mums had been seeing Tom and shooing him away as 'regular as clockwork'. The local relieving officer and a policeman were eventually persuaded to force an entry into Tom's house. Picking their way through the piles of junk and yellowing newspapers, they made their way upstairs and found him sitting up, but dead in his bed. Badly mutilated, his body was 'alive with vermin', which took some chasing off. He had been dead for months when they found him.

Even after Vinegar Tom was dead and buried, George swore that the shade of the bogeyman was still around – his wide brimmed hat and grotty coat caught out of the corner of your eye as he disappeared round the corner, his boots spotted shuffling along under the yard gate. You might not always have seen him, George said, but the sickly smell, unmistakable and unique to Tom, often wafted along the alleys of Cobholm. Perhaps it still does.

· Select Bibliography & Printed Sources ·

Blundell, Nigel and Boar, Roger *The World's Greatest Ghosts* (Octopus, 1983)

Day, J. Wentworth *Ghosts and Witches* (Batsford, 1954)

Dixon, G.M. *Folktales and Legends of Norfolk* (Minimax, 1980)

Glyde, John Jnr *Norfolk Garland* (Jarrold, 1872)

Haining, Peter *A Dictionary of Ghosts* (Hale, 1982)

Harries, John *The Ghost Hunter's Road Book* (Muller, 1968)

Hippisley Coxe, Antony D. *Haunted Britain* (Hutchinson, 1973)

Hole, Christina *Haunted England* (Batsford, 1951)

Howat, Polly *Norfolk Ghosts and Legends* (Countryside Books, 1993)

Jeffery, Peter *East Anglian Ghosts, Legends and Lore* (Old Orchard, 1988)

Mackie, Charles *Norfolk Annals* (Norfolk Chronicle, 1901)

Mitchell, John and Rickard, Robert J.M. *Phenomena: A Book of Wonders* (Thames & Hudson, 1977)

Sampson, Charles *Ghosts of the Broads* (Yachtsman, 1931)

Spencer, John and Anne *Ghost Hunters' Guide to Britain* (Harper Collins, 2000)

Storey, Neil R. *A Grim Almanac of Norfolk* (Sutton, 2003)

Storey, Neil R. *Norfolk Murders* (Sutton, 2006)

le Strange, Richard *Monasteries of Norfolk* (Yates, 1973)

Suffling, Ernest R. *The History and Legends of the Broad District* (Jarrold, 1891)

Thistleton-Dyer, T.F. *Ghost World* (Ward & Downey, 1893)
Westwood, Jennifer *Gothic Norfolk* (Shire, 1989)

Athenaeum
Country Life
East Anglian Magazine
Eastern Counties Collectanea
Eastern Daily Press
Norfolk Chronicle
Norfolk Fair
Norfolk Journal & East Anglian Life
Norfolk & Suffolk Notes & Queries
Paranormal Norfolk
Proceedings of the Society for Psychic Research
Strand Magazine
Yarmouth Mercury

Acknowledgements

It has been proved again that you can meet some of the nicest people when doing the grimmest research. There are too many to mention all by name, but I would particularly like to thank Andrew Selwyn-Crome, Jenny Bemment, Stewart P. Evans, James Nice, Chris Crease and Loddon & District Local History Group, Friends of Norwich & Norfolk Heritage, Helen Brumpton at the George Hotel, Swaffham, all our friends at Swaffham Museum, BBC Radio Norfolk, Walsingham Bridewell, The National Trust – Blickling Hall and Felbrigg Hall, Norwich Castle Museum, Tales of the Old Gaol House, King's Lynn, Friends of the Norfolk Dialect (FOND), *Norfolk Journal & East Anglian Life* and all my wonderful WEA students who have added their participation, encouragement and interest in the pursuit of the paranormal. Last but by no means least I thank my dear Mum who first kindled my interest in ghosts and, of course, my partner Molly and my son Lawrence for their love, thoughts and enthusiasm for exploring the places mentioned in this book.

• Index •